Standpoints

Svend Brinkmann

———

STANDPOINTS

10 Old Ideas in a New World

Translated by Tam McTurk

polity

First published in Danish as Ståsteder: 10 gamle ideer til en ny verden
© Svend Brinkmann & Gyldendal, Copenhagen 2016. Published by
agreement with Gyldendal Group Agency.

This English edition © Polity Press, 2018

Reprinted 2020

Polity Press
65 Bridge Street
Cambridge CB2 1UR, UK

Polity Press
101 Station Landing
Suite 300
Medford, MA 02155, USA

ISBN-13: 978-1-5095-2372-6
ISBN-13: 978-1-5095-2373-3(pb)

A catalogue record for this book is available from the British Library.

Typeset in 11 on 14 pt Sabon by
Servis Filmsetting Ltd, Stockport, Cheshire
Printed and bound in the United States by LSC Communications

The publisher has used its best endeavours to ensure that the URLs for
external websites referred to in this book are correct and active at the time
of going to press. However, the publisher has no responsibility for the
websites and can make no guarantee that a site will remain live or that the
content is or will remain appropriate.

Every effort has been made to trace all copyright holders, but if any have
been inadvertently overlooked the publisher will be pleased to include any
necessary credits in any subsequent reprint or edition.

For further information on Polity, visit our website: politybooks.com

To my mother and father

Contents

Preface   viii

Prologue: The Meaningful Life   1

1   The Good (Aristotle)   25

2   Dignity (Kant)   40

3   The Promise (Nietzsche)   52

4   The Self (Kierkegaard)   61

5   Truth (Arendt)   71

6   Responsibility (Løgstrup)   78

7   Love (Murdoch)   89

8   Forgiveness (Derrida)   100

9   Freedom (Camus)   110

10   Death (Montaigne)   123

Epilogue: Perspectives on the Meaning of Life   134

Notes   148

Preface

It is up to the reader to decide whether *Standpoints* works on its own, as a follow-up to *Stand Firm* (2017), or as both. At any rate, the book began to take shape while I was working on a radio series in Denmark. *Stand Firm* was wilfully humorous and adopted a sceptical approach to a number of contemporary social trends, in particular the constant demands for personal development and flexibility. But it left unanswered questions. If we are to stand firm and not bend with the wind, *on what* is it worth standing firm? And, if doing our duty – instead of always just doing what is best for us and our self-development – has some form of intrinsic value, then *of what* does duty consist? *Standpoints* is an attempt to answer these questions in a more constructive and edifying manner than was possible in *Stand Firm*, while remaining true to my critique of contemporary culture.

I should like to thank my editor Anne Weinkouff, whose help has been invaluable throughout the writing process. Following up on the widespread and surprising popularity of *Stand Firm* – both in Denmark and abroad – was a slightly daunting task, and Anne has been wonderfully supportive throughout. I should also like to thank the Danish Broadcasting Corporation and the Rosenkjær Committee, in particular the Chair, Anders Kinch-Jensen, for awarding me the prestigious science communication prize in 2015. I have thoroughly enjoyed working with various people at the Corporation. Huge thanks are also due to Ester Holte Kofod, Mikka Nielsen, Rasmus Birk, Anders Petersen and Thomas Aastrup Rømer for reading the manuscript and providing extremely helpful feedback. I should also like to thank Louise Knight of Polity Press and Tam McTurk, the translator, for all of their hard and excellent work on the English-language version. However, as always, my biggest thanks go to my wife, Signe Winther Brinkmann, *sine qua non*.

The book is dedicated to my parents, from whom I derive most of the standpoints on which I, personally, choose to stand firm.

Randers, Denmark
May 2017

Prologue:
The Meaningful Life

In 2014, at a press conference for his film *Magic in the Moonlight*, Woody Allen spoke in his customary pithy manner about the meaning of life:

> I firmly believe – and I don't say this as a criticism – that life is meaningless. I'm not saying that one should opt to kill oneself. But the truth of the matter is, when you think of it, every 100 years, there's a big flush, and everybody in the world is gone. And there's a new group of people. And that gets flushed, and there's a new group of people. And this goes on and on interminably – and I don't want to upset you – toward no particular end, no rhyme or reason. And the universe, as you know from the best of physicists, is coming apart, and eventually there will be nothing, absolutely nothing. All the great works of Shakespeare, and Beethoven, and Da Vinci, all that will be gone. Now, not for a long time, but shorter than you think, really, because the Sun is going to burn out much earlier than the universe vanishes.[1]

As a result, Allen went on, he has no interest in making political films, because 'while they do have current critical importance, in the large scheme of things, only the big questions matter, and the answers to those big questions are very, very depressing. What I would recommend – this is the solution that I've come up with – is distraction.'

The interview is full of the mixture of gravitas and humour for which Allen is so well known, but there is little doubt that he means what he says. And it is, of course, with a glint in his eye that the filmmaker extraordinaire recommends distractions – say, going to the cinema, for example – as a solution to life's dismal lack of meaning. The question is, however, whether Allen is right. Is life really meaningless? To justify his conviction that life has no meaning, he draws on physics – arguably the most objective of scientific perspectives and one far removed from everyday human concerns. He talks of the Sun as a star that will burn out, and about the creation and ultimate destruction of the whole universe. If we remove ourselves completely from the hurly-burly of day-to-day life and adopt a cosmological view, it should come as no surprise that it is impossible to detect any meaning in life. Everything just becomes physical material in motion, which seems a tad depressing. The famous psychologist William James (1842–1910), who was widely credited with introducing psychology to the United States (and, incidentally, brother to the author Henry James), thought that the depression he suffered in his youth had been triggered by studying science, which had taught him that the universe lacks meaning and humankind lacks free will. James' pragmatic solution was to choose to believe in free will and thus that individuals are capable of infusing their own lives with meaning. 'My first act of free will shall be to believe in free will', he wrote in his diary on 30 April 1870. James was convinced that this is what brought him out of his depression.

Not everyone possesses that level of mental fortitude. Most of us would shudder a little at Allen's words. Most of us are probably incapable of bestowing meaning and freedom on ourselves and our lives simply by *willing* it to be so. Instead, we might question whether it is actually reasonable to seek meaning in a sphere so far removed from day-to-day life, as Allen appears to do. What happens if we step *into* life to explore it from the inside, instead of stepping *out* of it to view it from an astronomical distance? The answer is that meaning becomes less problematic than Allen claims. For example, Allen's own words have meaning – whether or not we agree with them – and hopefully as a reader you will find this book quite meaningful. Perhaps meaning is a phenomenon only understood from the inside, and not from the outside, e.g. from the perspective of the physicist. After all, it goes without saying that the meaning of a poem is not grasped by weighing a poetry book or analysing the chemical composition of the ink on its pages.

So, in order to find meaning, we must delve into life rather than observe it from the outside. And what can we expect to find? My assertion is that we would, unfortunately, discover a lot of people who have difficulty defining the nature of meaning. The question seems to crop up more and more often these days – but answering it has probably never been more difficult. In material terms, we may be better off than ever before – we also live longer and treat illness and disease more effectively – but maybe many of us also lack meaning in our lives. The increasing frequency with which the question is asked, and the apparently never-ending stream of books on the subject, are not necessarily healthy signs. The very question itself – of the meaning of life – reflects an absence of something, a yearning. It is usually asked when people become aware of the lack of meaning in their lives. When our lives are busy – filled with family, friends, colleagues and all sorts of activity at work and in our spare time – the world seems loaded with significance and value. We rarely stop and ask ourselves whether it is 'meaningful' to make food for our kids, because making meals is, of course, an integral part of life. But when the normal pattern breaks down – when loved ones fall ill or die, or when restructuring or redundancies make our working lives difficult – we may find ourselves wondering about the meaning of it all. Why does whatever happens happen, and why do we do what we do? Is anything we do with our lives actually worthwhile?

Meaning and instrumentalisation

Other than adherents of fundamentalist creeds, most people find it impossible to come up with a definitive answer to the meaning of life. Nor does this book attempt to posit one. What it does offer is a suggestion for a direction that we might follow in order to relate to the question in a fruitful manner. In brief, the book's thesis is that meaning is derived from phenomena that constitute an end in themselves, and from activities we indulge in for their own sake, rather than to achieve or obtain something. These phenomena can only be discovered from within life itself, not from the objectifying, astronomical distance suggested by Woody Allen.

Prologue

In a conscious reference to my previous book, I have chosen to call phenomena that constitute ends in themselves 'standpoints'. They provide something on which to *stand firm* in a world in constant flux. Admittedly, the idea that meaning is bound up with phenomena that constitute ends in themselves is a view that is under considerable pressure from a social process that might be called *instrumentalisation*. Instrumentalisation, more than anything else, has made grappling with the question of meaning far more difficult. The concept refers to things becoming instruments – means or tools to achieving something else – and not, therefore, being ends in themselves. Increasingly, it feels as if most of what we do has become a means to an end, rather than having intrinsic value. Money is perhaps the most obvious instrumental phenomenon. It is used to buy food, a home, transport, clothes, holidays and so on – it pervades every aspect of modern life – but money has no value in itself. *Per se*, money is, of course, just paper and metal or information stored on a computer in a bank. However, as an instrument, money is a universal means of exchange, which, in principle, makes it possible to value everything and to compare it with everything else. The advent of a money-based economy was almost magical. Suddenly, it became possible to weigh everything on the same set of scales. Today, it is possible, for example, to translate an hour of talk (with a psychologist, coach or accountant) into a portion of mince or Cliff Richard's back catalogue. Money can be used to even out qualitative differences between objects and services and render all differences quantitative.

There is, of course, nothing wrong with instrumentalisation *per se*. Most of us would agree that using money is a better way to run our economy than a barter system, which would involve having to calculate how many apples correspond to a pair of shoes at any given point in time. In fact, most of us have a completely legitimate and somewhat instrumental relation to all sorts of things and activities – like sun cream and snow clearing. We do not apply sun cream because it is good *per se* to smear ourselves with it, but because we want to protect our skin against the Sun's harmful rays. Nor do we clear snow just for the sake of it. We want to be able to navigate the pavements without slipping and to drive safely in the winter. Instrumental activities and relations are completely fine, not to mention unavoidable. However, the dividing line between an instrumental understanding of life and one that is more value-based is not always very clear. This book is not engaged in a utopian endeavour to wipe out instrumentalism, but it does try to identify the problems that arise if instrumentalist thinking is our first port of call – or even the dominant one – as we relate to the world, other people and ourselves. And this, I believe, is becoming the case today. Again, money is an obvious example: it is such an all-pervasive phenomenon in modern life, and regulates so many facets of it, that we have a tendency to forget that money is actually a means and not an end in itself. The fact that relatively affluent people who lack nothing are willing to work themselves half to death (or worse) to amass even greater wealth is, of course, an obvious sign that they have turned a means into an end. People act as if money has intrinsic value, but it does not. So, what does? What does constitute an end in itself? The premise of this book is that if we answer that question – not necessarily once and for all, but at least as part of an ongoing existential discussion – then we are closer to understanding that which gives meaning to life.

I forget the source, but I once heard the following definition of art (which is, of course, almost as difficult to define as the meaning of life): art is there to remind us that there are things that are an end in themselves. Art reminds us of this because it is not possible to reduce its purpose to anything else without eliminating what is artistic about art. We might say that art is there to provide positive and beautiful experiences, but that makes art little more than a delivery mechanism for unadulterated wellness – and, of course, not all art is beautiful or agreeable. Or we might argue that art has a political purpose, but then it becomes propaganda – and, of course, not all art is political. Art can, of course, be both beautiful and political, but neither of these are its purpose. They are, at best, secondary effects because, in my opinion, the sole purpose of art is to be art.

Art is far from being the only form of self-expression that constitutes an end in itself. The same is true for example of ethical actions, of play and of love. Everything – including art, ethics, play and love – can *be made* a tool for something other than itself, as we will see in this book. This is, in a sense, the opposite of turning a means (e.g. money) into an end in itself – but both endeavours stem from confusion about what has intrinsic value. For example, modern employers often instrumentalise play, making it a means of generating innovative ideas and facilitating the exercise of soft power.[2] Something that used to belong solely to our free time has become a management tool to generate profit. It is, of course, an open question whether this is still play – because play can, by definition, be said to be free and not driven by another purpose. Can it be instrumentalised and still be play? We do not usually play to earn money or make a company competitive; we play to play. Otherwise these activities are not play at all, but work or profit maximisation. Profit maximisation is a legitimate endeavour, but can hardly be said to be an end in itself. I am not claiming that all instrumentalisation is odious or reprehensible – of course not. However, I would argue that it is now so all-pervasive that it threatens other ways of thinking that are far more fundamental to our ability to live well and meaningfully. Instrumentalisation can all too easily obscure that which is actually meaningful.

The useful

Instrumentalisation is an offshoot of utilitarianism. In modern society, we prefer to use the means or instruments that provide the best return – in other words, the ones that are the most useful. This is so ingrained in our culture that we are often blind to the pitfalls. Politicians in most countries have long sought to maximise the 'bang for our buck' – we want to get the most for our money, be it in health, environmental measures or education. Let us take education as an example. The idea of 'maximum learning for our money' often means that nurseries and schools opt for whatever educational practices have been proven, in meta-analyses of research results, to provide the best quantifiable return. Decision-makers minimise the significance of decades (even centuries) of tradition in child-rearing and teaching. The role of the teacher or nursery assistant is radically transformed from someone who exercises professional judgement to a conduit for the intentions of researchers and civil servants. It is also an approach that ignores the importance of local context (country, region, town, district, school year) in favour of a generalised insight into 'what works'. In reality, of course, none of this actually 'works', because tradition, the individual involved and the context play far too great a role in all forms of education. The real problem is that we allow ourselves to believe that it works. The consequence of this is that we seek to reduce things that do have some kind of value *per se* – i.e. the content and wider historical and cultural context in which the field of education is necessarily rooted – to an instrument fine-tuned to achieve certain results in national tests and PISA rankings. It has become a goal in itself for pupils to achieve good test results for comparative purposes – even though these results are, at best, a means (of evaluating political targets) and never an end in themselves. What good is a high PISA ranking (the statistical value of which, incidentally, is highly debatable[3]) if it has only been achieved by pupils training specifically to take the test and sit exams, rather than immersing themselves in the subject in all its complexity? It transforms the means (tests and rankings) into an end *per se*, while the actual end (academic knowledge and a democratic mindset) falls by the wayside. Turning means into ends is one of the most damaging trends in modern society. In the eyes of the system, the value of childhood is reduced to churning out pupils who achieve the right results and preparing them to be 'soldiers in the competition state', as one political scientist put it.[4] In other words, in our modern era, even childhood is subjected to instrumentalisation. It is merely a means to foster an effective and innovative workforce, so the nation can cope in a competitive global economy.

Instrumental psychology and useless philosophy

The utility value of the humanities is frequently discussed these days. In an instrumentalised and utilitarian era, humanities subjects face all kinds of challenges. What do history, drama studies or French do for GDP and national competitiveness? What use are they? One of the basic premises of this book is a paradox: namely that many disciplines – including the humanities – are of use precisely by virtue of their uselessness. In other words, it is more important than ever to show that there is more to life than what is 'useful'. Accepting this is, therefore, useful in a deeper and more existential way. In this sense, art, play, love and ethics are at their most useful when they are useless – that is, when they do not serve any purpose, when they are ends in themselves. Following this line of argument, it is the supposedly useless phenomena that give life content and meaning. The humanities are important precisely because they deal with phenomena like art, ethics, etc.

I am a psychologist. Ours is a particularly interesting discipline because it has one foot in the humanities and the other in the natural sciences. Some aspects of psychology study human beings as creatures who act and suffer, who live in culture's historical world of signs and symbols, while other aspects study human beings as physiological entities, as constructions of central nervous systems, genes and hormones that function according to the principle of cause and effect. On a personal level, I find both aspects fascinating and legitimate. However, since the book is concerned with meaning, the first set of phenomena are more important here.

The fact that the book centres around philosophy rather than psychology has to do with the fact that – more or less since its inception as a science in the late nineteenth century – psychology has unfortunately played a role in the process of social instrumentalisation. We might, in a slightly whimsical way, say that psychology has been the instrument of this instrumentalisation. It has been one of the most important means by which instrumentalisation has taken hold. What does this mean? It means, for example, that psychology, by dint of its cultural status as a modern 'ersatz religion', has offered individuals a range of tools that supposedly enable them to 'work on themselves'.[5] Psychology has transformed the religious goal of salvation into self-realisation; confession and pastoral care have become therapy and coaching; the modern secular priesthood consists of psychologists and self-help gurus; and God's place at the centre of the cosmos has been usurped by the self. This has happened over the last couple of centuries. However, unlike the religious idea of the divine and the absolute as ends in themselves, psychology – to put it somewhat simply – offers means without ends. Or at least without ends other than those derived from the individual's subjective self – or from national targets for 'skills enhancement'. Psychology's means range from psychotherapy, coaching, appreciative inquiry (AI), positive thinking, mindfulness and nonviolent communication (NVC) at the soft humanities end, to intelligence and personality tests at the hard natural science end. Many of these means have been incorporated into our self-understanding and institutions, where we have attempted to transform them into ends in themselves. For example, we now believe that there is intrinsic value in authenticity ('being yourself'), acting on the basis of 'gut feelings' or achieving a certain result in a psychological test. However, it is easy to show that these phenomena do not have intrinsic value. Imagine that you 'find yourself' only to discover that you are, in fact, a cruel and heartless monster. Would being somebody else not be preferable, even if it meant being a less authentic version of you? As I argued in *Stand Firm*, it is better to be a good (moral) person than to be yourself. This is because goodness, as an ethical value, must be considered an end in itself, whereas being your authentic self is, at best, a means to being a good person (and at worst, serves as a barrier to this). It would, of course, be great to be both good and yourself at one and the same time. But if you have to choose, you ought to opt for goodness, as it is the only one of the two with intrinsic value.

In short, my criticism of psychology is that, while it may have been excellent at helping individuals develop and 'become themselves' through the use of diverse psychological tools (the means), it has not been particularly good at creating an ethical and social upbringing (the ends).[6] As one late-twentieth-century book put it in its title, *We've Had a Hundred Years of Psychotherapy and the World's Getting Worse*.[7] Psychology has arguably been far too useful in terms of instrumentalising personal development, learning and self-realisation, while totally neglecting 'the useless' – that which serves no practical purpose, but which is an end in itself. As such, psychology – or at least some of it – has contributed not just to the instrumentalisation of society but also to a self-centred culture and, in certain cases, outright narcissism.

In the rest of the book, I will therefore mainly use philosophical ideas to express a non-instrumental way of thinking that is useful precisely because it is useless. My hope is that psychology will increasingly absorb philosophical ideas – but this will require psychology allowing itself to draw inspiration from philosophy, as indeed it did when it was a very new science. If everything in the modern world has to be useful, then only the useless is actually useful in helping us (re)discover meaning. And I cannot find any discipline, any method of thinking, that is more useless – and therefore necessary – than philosophy. Well, maybe art, but since I know a lot more about philosophy, this is where I will focus my efforts.

But what do I mean by philosophy? Defining where philosophy ends and psychology starts (and vice versa) is by no means straightforward. In one sense, all sciences (including psychology) stem from philosophy, and defining philosophy is, in itself, a huge philosophical conundrum. This book seeks to use philosophical ideas to formulate a philosophy of life capable of resisting instrumentalisation and utilitarian thinking. Part of that project consists of reflecting on what philosophy actually *is*. I will begin with the simple definition suggested by the famous American philosopher Stanley Cavell. Philosophy, he says, is 'education for grownups'.[8] In other words, one way of understanding philosophy is as part of the process of upbringing, education and ethical formation. Once we grow up and start to reflect on life, death, love and other big existential themes, philosophy helps contextualise our thinking as part of a practical project of self-education. This process of contextualising our thinking is an absolute prerequisite for resisting instrumentalisation and approaching the question of the meaningful life from the correct perspective. Philosophy helps us to dig deeper and undermine established truths, to keep asking awkward questions where sciences like psychology have fallen short. 'We can measure happiness with a questionnaire', says the psychologist, 'and this makes it possible to optimise well-being and make people more productive!' 'But is that really happiness?' asks the philosopher. 'Is it really meaningful?' The philosopher keeps digging, asking questions that are always apposite and critical.

Philosophy may offer a means of contextualising our thinking, but in my opinion it should do so with a practical aim. The purpose of philosophical reflection, as formulated by historian of philosophy Pierre Hadot, is to be able to live 'the philosophical life'.[9] In modern university departments, philosophy is an analytical discipline, but originally – in Greek antiquity – it was a way of life. This perhaps applied most clearly to ethics (which help individuals to live well) and politics (which help build a good society), but logic was also seen as a practical tool with which to foster the development of clear thinking, while physics (a sub-discipline of philosophy at the time) was seen as a contemplative practice concerned with the place of humankind in the cosmos. This book attempts to rehabilitate philosophy as a way of life that helps us reflect on what constitutes a meaningful life. The original goal of all of the classical schools of philosophy (Platonism, Epicureanism, Stoicism, Cynicism, etc.) was *paideia* (the rearing, education and ethical formation of the ideal citizen) – in other words, helping us live with our human nature. This was an endeavour with intrinsic value, as it was not a means to an end. Education (*paideia*) was its own end.

According to Plato and many of the philosophers who followed in his footsteps, philosophy (which literally means love of wisdom) stems from wonder. We wonder why there is something rather than nothing, why there is evil if God is both good and omniscient, what makes the good *good* – and when we do, we are starting to philosophise. Children also ask these questions, which partially contradicts Cavell's definition of philosophy as education for grown-ups. On the other hand, it probably requires an adult intellect to think philosophically – to examine your concepts, ask clearer questions and express the answers more accurately. Plato's starting point – that philosophy stems from wonder – is not wrong, but I personally believe that the approach advocated by the contemporary philosopher Simon Critchley is at least equally valid. For Critchley, philosophy stems from disappointment:[10] on the one hand, disappointment that justice is not accorded to us. He writes that we live in a 'violent, unjust world', in which it is seldom the good who win in the end, and in which tyrants sometimes live happily ever after. The disappointment that arises from this lack of justice leads to political philosophy and the desire to strive for a better society. On the other hand, according to Critchley, philosophy stems from disappointment that there is no God. This also echoes Woody Allen's starting point – a universe in which there is no guarantor of meaning. Everything may just be mere cosmic coincidence or a manifestation of nature's blind forces.

In the late nineteenth century, Nietzsche earned fame by responding to the loss of God and, therefore, of meaning. He acknowledged that the loss of God could lead directly to nihilism – in other words, not just to inquisitive questions about the meaning of life, but to an explicit assertion, and perhaps even worship, of meaninglessness. Contrary to popular belief, this was not Nietzsche's own attitude. Rather, he was preoccupied with formulating a response to the threat of nihilism and its cultural implications. Nihilists claim that all values are groundless and, therefore, hollow. Nietzsche wanted to reassess the nature of values (especially Christian ones) in order to protect humankind from a nihilistic catastrophe.

The threat of nihilism

This book is not Nietzschean, but it does share his concern about nihilism and culture. Our contemporary instrumentalisation of society is in effect nihilistic, as it does not allow anything to be an end in itself. Let me give some examples. No matter how we might feel about an institution like the royal family in a modern constitutional monarchy, it is in my opinion thought-provoking how often it is defended on the grounds that the royals are assumed to generate profit for the nation. But why does the economic argument carry so much weight in this context? Should all institutions be judged solely on the basis of their cash value? Ultimately, all utilitarian thinking is nihilistic, because it does not allow for anything to have intrinsic value. It is easy enough to come up with quite grotesque illustrations of this: a recent article in one of the Danish Sunday papers revealed that sorting our own household waste prior to recycling allegedly makes us happy. But, we might ask, why is that even relevant? Is this not something that we should be doing anyway, whether or not it makes us happy? And while money is nice to have, it is actually nihilistic in the proper sense of the term, because it reduces qualitative differences to quantitative ones. In a monetary system, everything is weighed on the same set of scales.

But how do we overcome nihilism if we no longer have God as our guarantor of meaning?[11] Of course, people still refer to gods, but many of us (including yours truly) find the notion of a deity an unsatisfactory answer to the meaning of life. Claiming that meaning exits because a god exists just avoids the question of what the meaningful consists of.[12] This is in no way an argument against religious faith, merely an underlining of the fact that referring to a deity does not automatically answer the question of meaning. The questions about God's existence and about meaningfulness are, in principle, completely different. For example, God could have created a universe devoid of meaning, as some existentialist theologians would claim. Meaning without God and God without meaning are both perfectly conceivable.

Critchley differentiates between two forms of nihilism that arise in the wake of a loss of cultural meaning. The first is an active nihilism, which responds to meaninglessness by calling for the destruction of the world as we know it and the creation of a new one. Active nihilism is political, and its purest form manifests itself in terror groups like Baader-Meinhof, the Red Brigades or, more topically, those now operating under names like al-Qaeda and Islamic State. Their violent logic is that the modern capitalist world is meaningless and therefore must be destroyed and replaced with a (communist/ religious) Utopia. But there is also a passive form of nihilism, which is far more widespread in the general population. In order to come to terms with emptiness and meaninglessness, the passive nihilist, as Critchley puts it, 'withdraws to an island'. He mentions 'European Buddhism' as one example of passive nihilism, referring to how, in the West, this Eastern tradition often becomes a form of self-centred self-development. The knowledge that nothing outside of the self has meaning leads passive nihilists to focus on 'the inner world', on their own psychology and self-development, based on what 'feels right inside'. Things are deemed to be good because they 'feel good' for the individual and deemed bad when they 'feel wrong'. Passive nihilism is therefore a form of pure subjectivism, which reduces all of the world's many diverse processes and characteristics to their psychological effect upon the individual, an effect the individual is expected to master – making him or her something akin to a god. This is why, as mentioned above, the self has usurped God's place as the centre of the universe. We mistakenly believe that meaning is the same as the individual's experience of happiness. However, many people sense the hollowness in this, and perhaps feel like Estragon in Samuel Beckett's famous absurd play *Waiting for Godot*, when he says: 'We are happy. (Silence) What do we do now, now that we are happy?' And Vladimir replies: 'Wait for Godot.'[13] What we call happiness these days is perhaps not the same as meaning, because happiness is often understood in a subjectivist sense, based on psychological categories such as 'subjective well-being' or 'self-realisation'. Conversely, one of the basic points in this book is that the meaningful is not subjective, or something 'internal', but is derived from phenomena – standpoints – in our lives as part of a society.

We have now established that overcoming instrumentalisation and resisting nihilism are two sides of the same coin. As mentioned previously, this book's starting point is that this process of overcoming instrumentalisation needs to have a practical dimension in our everyday lives, rather than be a purely theoretical approach, if we are to relate to meaning in a non-nihilistic way. But how do we achieve this? Both religious texts and modern self-help literature excel at providing practical advice, usually by offering succinct maxims to remember and by which to live our lives. To use the technical term, these maxims function as 'symbolic resources' – in other words, small cultural fragments we use to regulate our thoughts, emotions or actions.[14] When faced with a difficult choice, a Christian might ask 'What would Jesus do?' and use the idealised Christ as a symbolic resource. Or we might hum a tune, using it as a symbolic resource to reassure ourselves, e.g. if we feel scared walking home alone in the dark.

In *Stand Firm*, I caricatured self-help literature with my own seven-step guide to avoiding dependency on interminable development and flexibility. When writing the book, I found it liberating to be direct and pithy. This book does not use the seven-step structure. It presents ten ideas by ten philosophers from different epochs and starting points, which will hopefully serve as symbolic resources for the modern individual who is interested in meaning. *Stand Firm* was an explicit critique of society, which contained a more implicit discussion about the meaning and value of life. *Standpoints*, conversely, makes the meaningful explicit, while the social critique is more implicit (usually taking the form of critical comments about contemporary instrumentalisation). In general, the concept of 'standpoints' refers to tangible places and ideas to which we are linked and from which we derive stimulation. I should like to have written more directly about actual physical places in this book, but my concept of 'standpoints' is more metaphorical, and refers to 'oases' as it were, places where meaning can arise because a phenomenon is allowed to manifest itself in all its inherent value. In our modern, instrumentalised meritocracy, some will see these ten standpoints as somewhat utopian, but I see them as a stark contrast to the utopian ideal. 'Utopia' stems from the Greek world for 'no place', whereas standpoints do actually exist in our lives. We just need to be reminded of them and learn to relate to them without resorting to instrumentalist thinking.

These ten ideas are, therefore, intended as reminders of what is important and meaningful in life. My hope is that they will help you realise that there are some things that have value in and of themselves and are an intrinsic part of a meaningful human existence. In other words, the book presents ten elements of a philosophy of life, covering ten different existential themes or phenomena, on which modern human beings might usefully reflect in order to overcome nihilism and instrumentalisation. Some readers will, with a certain degree of justification, accuse me of eclecticism, of combining completely different ideas by taking elements from a highly diverse

group of thinkers and arranging them in a philosophical mosaic. Does this not run the risk of destroying the
uniqueness of each thinker? Well, yes, it does. And this
book is not for those seeking in-depth and well-rounded
analyses of the individual philosophers' thinking. Nor
should you expect the ten standpoints to form some
kind of higher synthesis out of the disparate schools
of thought from which the elements stem. Rather, you
should see the ten chapters as a source of existential
inspiration for reflection on the meaning of life in our
modern age. I would add, however, that I believe that
while we often think of philosophers as belonging to
distinct, compartmentalised 'schools', they are often
very much in dialogue with each other. To a significant
extent, they talk about the same themes and phenomena.
This, I think, supports the underlying aim of this book:
to find ten basic philosophical themes that will help us
formulate standpoints for an anti-instrumentalist thinking. I believe that these themes allow us to make out the
rough contours of a philosophical anthropology that
portrays humans as interconnected beings with obligations, who are reared and educated in our encounters
with something other than the self. These humans do
not become themselves solely as a result of introspective
self-insight, but just as much via what I would call 'self-
outsight' – directed, not least, towards the basic values
represented in the ten chapters in this book.

The structure of the book

Each of the existential themes is covered in a short chapter, in which I attempt to explain the thinking behind

them and how the ideas relate to trends in our day and age. Hopefully, the ten ideas will be useless in a useful way, in the sense that they will convey an understanding of the concept that it is rarely the useful that is meaningful. The ten ideas might be said to express basic existential conditions on which we can stand firm because they have intrinsic value. They are:

1. The Good: If there is something we do for its own sake, it must be the overall good (Aristotle).
2. Dignity: Everything has either a price or dignity (Kant).
3. The Promise: Man is an animal with the right to make promises (Nietzsche).
4. The Self: The self is a relation that relates to itself (Kierkegaard).
5. Truth: Although there is no truth, man can be truthful (Arendt).
6. Responsibility: The individual never has anything to do with another person without holding something of this person's life in his hand (Løgstrup).
7. Love: Love is the extremely difficult realisation that something other than oneself is real (Murdoch).
8. Forgiveness: Forgiveness forgives only the unforgivable (Derrida).
9. Freedom: Freedom is not constituted primarily of privileges but of responsibilities (Camus).
10. Death: He who has learned to die has unlearned to serve (Montaigne).

After introducing each of the ten ideas, I will present an overview of what they teach us about living a meaningful life. The reader should not expect a single answer to the question of what constitutes a meaningful life. Instead, I will explore ways in which the question can be discussed and point to existential themes that act as essential components of a meaningful life in an otherwise thoroughly instrumentalised era.

The ten ideas are borrowed from philosophers and often formulated as maxims – relatively short sentences that you can learn off by heart and keep in mind as you go through life. I think that these ideas are extremely relevant to the age in which we live. Old ideas are not bad just because they are old. The fact that the old ideas presented in this book are boiled down into short maxims is in keeping with classical philosophy as a way of life. The ideas are conveyed via what Hadot calls special systematics, which 'provide the mind with a small number of principles, tightly linked together, which derived greater persuasive force and mnemonic effectiveness from such systematization' – in other words, they are easy to remember.[15] In his famous book on philosophy as a way of life, in which he rediscovers classical philosophy's idea of education, Hadot underlines time and time again that we need aphorisms, maxims and short summaries of the wisdom that is existentially significant for humankind.

The ten ideas in this book are a catalogue of such maxims, designed to help readers relate the thinking behind them to their own lives and arrive at an understanding of what is existentially important and meaningful. Our minds are often full of jingles, pop songs and bits of adverts, but if you are interested in meaning and philosophy as a way of life, you may find it relevant to incorporate some of these ten ideas (or any others that appeal to you) into an ongoing process of reflection. The book can, of course, be read chronologically, but you should also be able to benefit from jumping around and reading about the ideas that interest you most. The chapters are short and do not take long to read. Hopefully, you will spend more time thinking about the ideas in them than reading about them.

After reading this book, you should hopefully be able to answer the question of what standpoints are worth standing firm on in your life. You should be able to counter Woody Allen's dispiriting assertion that ultimately nothing has any meaning. His films may offer a wonderful form of distraction, but you should also understand that there are other ways of protecting yourself against meaninglessness – perhaps you will even come to realise that the desire for distraction is part of the problem, rather than the solution. Hopefully, the book will also give you ammunition for political discussions about the direction you would prefer society to take. While it is beyond the remit of politicians in any country to design a meaningful life for their citizens, I believe that we should discuss how the current wave of instrumentalisation threatens the meaning and value of life. Above all else, the ideas presented in the book are conceived as ways of gaining what I call 'self-outsight'. Not because self-insight is of no importance, but because it is predicated on the ability to look outside the self, at human standpoints.

1

The Good

If there is something we do for its own sake, it must be the overall good.

Aristotle (384–322 BCE)

I am an aficionado of the in-flight magazine. Sitting nervously, strapped into a tiny little seat and forbidden to go online, one of the few distractions is the magazine wedged deliberately in the pocket in front of you. The September 2015 edition of the SAS magazine *Scandinavian Traveler* was devoted to 'the good', which attracted my attention and piqued my philosophical curiosity. 'The Good Issue', as this edition was called, was full of articles about goodness, in many different forms. The most illuminating was probably the article on research, which explored the question posed by its title: 'Why be good?'[1] Why should we be morally good? Although this is a question with which many of the great thinkers have wrestled over the millennia, the article does not cite any of them, preferring instead to refer to contemporary psychology. It posits five answers, each of which is based on giving something to others, and alleges that they are supported by psychological and scientific literature (including brain research). The article says that we should be good because (1) giving makes us feel happy, (2) when we give, we receive, (3) giving evokes gratitude, (4) giving is good for our health, and (5) giving is contagious – it inspires others to do the same.

Apart from the final reason, which at least involves something other than psychological benefits for the giver, each of the reasons is instrumental – it is about what we *get out of* giving. They are also subjectivist and egocentric, in that they refer to what we *ourselves* get out of it. In short, giving makes us happy and healthy. Good news, of course, but is that really why we should be good? Aristotle, the first of the great anti-instrumentalist thinkers presented in this book, would doubtless respond in the negative: there are things that we ought to do irrespective of whether we ourselves will get something out of it. According to Aristotle, not everything can be measured quantitatively on scales of happiness and health. If we do something that has intrinsic value (e.g. being kind to others), it has a form of meaning and dignity in itself – regardless of the consequences for our own health, happiness or well-being. In our age of instrumentalisation, people's first instinct when called upon to do something is often to ask 'what's in it for me?' – rather than to think about what is worth doing.

The first standpoint upon which, I would suggest, it is worth standing firm is more or less the opposite of the vision of goodness expressed in *Scandinavian Traveler* – and perpetuated throughout society. It is an overarching thesis that underpins the other ideas, and that is why I think it is important to start with it, although there are many other good reasons to start with Aristotle, as he and Plato (427–347 BCE) are probably the most important thinkers in the history of Western philosophy. I will not dwell on Aristotle's biography. This book is not about the history of philosophy, after all. However, it is worth mentioning that he studied at Plato's Academy in Athens and that, following the death of his mentor, Aristotle tutored Alexander the Great and went on to found his own school of philosophy. His works, which deal with virtually every scientific and philosophical question, were forgotten in the West for hundreds of years following the fall of the Roman Empire, but were rediscovered thanks to the Arab scholars who had preserved his writings. During the Middle Ages, the big intellectual challenge consisted of reconciling Aristotle's science and philosophy with Christianity.

Despite their master/pupil relationship, there were major differences between Plato and Aristotle. In his dialogues, through the voice of Socrates, Plato advocated a philosophy that posited an ideal world of eternal, immutable ideas – which he called *forms* – of which the world as we experience it is merely a pale reflection. He also believed in the immortality of the soul. For Aristotle, however, the body and soul are inextricably linked (the soul is the form of the living body), and therefore the soul ceases to exist when the body dies. He formulated a doctrine in which material substances consist of forms (or ideas) that manifest themselves *in* matter, whereas Plato saw forms as existing in an eternal realm that lies *beyond* matter. The difference was encapsulated by the Renaissance painter Raphael in his famous *The School of Athens* (1509), which depicts a gathering of all of the great ancient philosophers, with Plato and Aristotle in the middle. Plato points upwards towards the eternal ideas, while Aristotle stretches out his hand in an attempt to touch the worldly. His motto might have been 'have faith in the Earth' – an idea not articulated until a couple of millennia later by Nietzsche.

Thus, while Plato, with his aesthetically appealing dialogues, has inspired many artists and poets (despite his notorious scepticism about poetry), Aristotle has inspired science, logic and rational thinking. Aristotle was in many ways the originator of the various sciences and the distinctions between them. He was an observant natural scientist, who considered humankind to be a social species like swans and bees, but also acknowledged that we are a uniquely political and rational animal. Humans are therefore not solely governed by their instincts. By exercising judgement, we are capable of deciding what is the right thing to do in a given situation. We are not solely driven by biological impulses. Other good reasons motivate us too, including ethical ones. However, we are only capable of this once we have learned to do so – in other words, when we have had our character shaped and we have acquired virtues within an organised political community, or *polis* (the Greek city state). As the Greeks put it, *Polis andra didaske* ('man is shaped by the city') – we are only human in a real sense if we are provided with a stable social structure in which to form our character. The question is then whether our modern instrumentalised culture offers such a structure or *polis*.

So what does Aristotle have to do with instrumentalisation and our question about meaning and value? The answer is that he, more than any other philosopher, was responsible for founding an anti-instrumentalist way of thinking that is still relevant to this day. We might even go as far as to say that his understanding of human-kind is linked to a kind of anti-instrumentalism. To paraphrase the introduction to his famous book *The Nicomachean Ethics*: all human endeavour is thought to aim at some good. While the purpose of some activities lies outside the activities themselves, other activities are for their own sake. If it is true that not all of our activities are instrumental (in other words, aimed at achieving something other than the activity itself), it must be possible to identify what we do for its own sake – and this must then be the overall good. '[The] end of the medical art is health, that of shipbuilding a vessel, that of strategy victory, that of economics wealth', he writes.[2] We might extrapolate from this and ask whether health, victory and wealth are also means, or whether they are ends in themselves.

The Nicomachean Ethics originally served as a manuscript for lectures designed to shape Aristotle's audiences into good people and citizens. It is a study of what constitutes the good in life – *eudaimonia* – and of the virtues and human characteristics needed to achieve this state. Aristotle asks: Which characteristics do we need in order for us to participate in those activities that are undertaken for their own sake? How are these characteristics developed? And – not least – what are these activities? If it is true, as I argued in the Prologue, that a meaningful life is best understood as one in which we engage in activities with intrinsic value, then Aristotle's ethics are ultimately about what constitutes a meaningful life and how to live one.

Eudaimonia *and the virtues*

Aristotle's answer to the question of what activities we indulge in for their own sake points mainly in the direction of what we might call ethical actions. The meaningful and flourishing life – *eudaimonia* – is one in which we do good deeds. Good deeds are an end in themselves and fundamental to *eudaimonia*. What makes a deed good (for example, helping somebody in need) is not the honour, fame or money attributed to the person who does it – although these may well be among its outcomes – but the fact that the action is good *per se*. The human virtues (practical reason, courage, moderation, etc.) are thus the traits that make us capable of doing good deeds. Aristotle's concept of virtue is therefore completely different from modern talk of a 'virtuous person', which has an old-fashioned, almost prudish ring to it. Aristotelian virtues are closer to our psychological concept of personality traits or character, only seen from a perspective that evaluates ethically.

As well as good deeds in an ethical sense, Aristotle also identifies contemplation as an end in itself. Humans are rational animals, so it is hardly surprising that it is when we deploy our unique powers to reason and to define that we live a meaningful life. According to Aristotle, reason is both practical (when it translates into good deeds) and theoretical (when contemplating existential and cosmic questions). The contemplative element may sound strange, but it is actually quite simple. Many non-scientists enjoy TV programmes about science (physics, biology, etc.). I often watch them with my children. In all probability, neither I nor the kids will

30

ever 'use' the knowledge that we acquire, but there is something fundamentally salutary and significant about being introduced to the complexities of the origins and evolution of the universe, the evolution of the species and humanity's place in the cosmos. One of my favourite books is *A Short History of Nearly Everything*, by the popular non-fiction writer Bill Bryson – not because it is exceptionally thorough or profound (self-evidently not, as it relates the whole history of the universe in one easily accessible book), but because reading it makes us appreciate the universe in all its myriad complexity, as well as the happy coincidence that we, ourselves, are part of it. Aristotle would probably say that it is precisely the 'uselessness' of this knowledge that is the best thing about it, because it is knowledge acquired for its own sake, and not in order to achieve something else. Watching science programmes or reading Bryson's book are examples of the type of practices also cultivated by the later Stoic philosophers, who sought to acknowledge that we are all part of a greater whole (the cosmos).[3] This acknowledgement or knowledge has no other purpose than acknowledgement itself, in the same way that ethical actions ought not to have any other purpose than the actions themselves. This is one of the key points in Aristotle: the good is defined as that which has its own intrinsic value. In this sense, the good consists of the useless – which, paradoxically, can be seen as useful precisely because it is useless. The following nine chapters identify other useless phenomena and define them as existential standpoints in a meaningful life.

One way to understand Aristotle's ancient, and potentially quite alien, idea of uselessness is to look at his book about ethics. It includes an analysis of friendship and its importance in life. Aristotle distinguishes between three types of friendship – the useful (based on utility), the pleasurable, and the noble (based on goodness). A clear example of friendship based on utility would be our relationship to contacts on LinkedIn, the purpose of which is professional networking – an inherently utilitarian pursuit. This is a purely instrumental relationship because it only has value if there is something in it, if it is mutually beneficial. The relationship has no intrinsic value, only utilitarian value. Friendships based on pleasure are similar, only the motivation is the individual's craving for pleasant and pleasurable experiences. We enter into relationships because they are fun and entertaining – once that stops being the case, they lose their justification. According to Aristotle, relationships based on utility and pleasure cannot be friendships in the proper sense, because they are defined in solely instrumental terms. Noble friendships, on the other hand, are motivated by the wish that things will go well for the other party – not by 'what's in it for me' (be it utility or pleasure). In other words, noble – or *real* – friendships are good *per se*. Aristotle writes convincingly that it is probably impossible to have very many friends of this type. If we have 500 'friends' on Facebook, very few will be the real thing. We may well get something out of having a friend (including both utility and pleasure), but that is not what defines the relationship as a friendship. We also derive utility from tradespeople, e.g. if we are not capable of laying tiles ourselves, and we derive aesthetic pleasure from watching a ballet dancer. But this does not make the tradesperson or dancer our friend.

The instrumental values (utility and pleasure) are, to use the philosophical concept, *accidental*. This means that they *can* result from friendships (or many other things), if we are lucky, but instrumental values do not define friendships. What does define them is that they have intrinsic value. They are, to use another philosophical term, *essential*. Similarly, it is *accidental* that schoolchildren learn to read better if they exercise for forty-five minutes a day,[4] but it is *essential* that physical beings exercise in general. Humans are probably the only species capable of real friendship, i.e. a relationship based solely on wishing the best for the other party, no matter what is in it for us. Many other species have complex social relationships based on dominance and raising their offspring, and some readers will perhaps be sceptical about the human potential for non-instrumental relationships. A nihilist, for example, will say that friendship is meaningless *per se*, but we still get something out of it. However, Aristotle insisted that non-instrumental relationships are possible, and that it is a defining characteristic of humankind that we have them. Without them, we are little more than advanced apes.

Modern subjectivism

Most people these days would not share Aristotle's view of what is good and meaningful. Many of us tend more towards the nihilist or subjectivist position, and think that questions of value, quality and meaning are, in the final analysis, subjective – if indeed they exist at all. From this perspective, no friendship is more real than any other. If I define friendship as being based on utility or pleasure, then that is what friendship means to me!

For the nihilist, it is up to the individual to decide what constitutes a good and meaningful life, and what counts as a meaningful relationship with others. However, if the question of what is good were really just a matter of taste, then subjectivism would be correct. It would be the case, as famously espoused by the liberal economist Milton Friedman, that, when it comes to fundamental differences over basic values, 'men can ultimately only fight'. Conversely, if Aristotle is right that some things are good irrespective of whether the individual subjectively acknowledges it, then subjectivism is wrong. It opens up the possibility of discussing values with each other rationally, rather than fighting about them and forcing our subjective attitudes on others.

According to Aristotelian philosophy, subjectivism is wrong because everything is defined by its purpose. For example, a heart (as we now know) is a muscle, the purpose of which is to pump blood around the body and supply cells with oxygen and sustenance. The nature of the heart's function is not a question of subjective taste. With the knowledge we possess today, nobody could rationally say 'I don't think that the heart is a pump' – because that is just what it is. In a similar vein, a knife is defined by its ability to cut things and a clock by its ability to tell us the time. In much the same way, Aristotle thought that human beings are defined by their purpose. A good person is one who has fulfilled their purpose and does that which, according to their nature, they ought to do. We have already seen that for Aristotle, humans are rational beings who possess the ability to deploy both practical and theoretical rationality – and therefore both act and think well – and because this defines us, our purpose is to act in accordance with these capabilities. We now begin to understand Aristotle's view of the virtues a bit better, i.e. as the characteristics that make us human. I should learn to think and act rationally not because 'it's just who I am!' but because being rational is an inherent part of being human. We should learn to think rationally even if 'it just isn't me!' I mentioned previously that refining the ability to think and act rationally is only something that can be achieved within the framework of an organised society (*polis*). It is not something that can be demanded of the individual as an isolated being – and in this context, education, upbringing and how we are reared in general are, of course, absolutely crucial. We need to learn to think rationally. But it is important to understand that what constitutes reason is not a matter of taste. For example, it would not be rational to say 'I don't think logic is valid.' Aristotle's concept of reason encompasses logic, but also so much more. There are more or less rational ways to think, feel and act, based, to varying degrees, on the situations we encounter throughout our lives. It may be a matter of discussion whether this or that is rational, but if we are to take Aristotle seriously then it is indisputably the case that reason transcends subjectivity – especially given that by its nature discussion must consist of an exchange of rational arguments if it is not to descend into verbal mudslinging. It is not up to the individual to define either their own purpose or what has intrinsic value.

Today, many contend that ethics, morals, values and even the meaning of life are all subjective matters, which perhaps explains why instrumentalism has such a firm grip on our culture and society. Because if it is possible to reduce meaning to mere subjective taste (which ends up being a form of nihilism) then we ought merely to develop instruments that allow us to realise our own subjective tastes to the greatest possible extent. Knowledge, ethics, friendship, trust, recognition and other phenomena are then there purely for the individual's sake, and are endowed with value relative to the individual's taste, i.e. whether he or she likes it or not. Knowledge is good if I like it (or can use it for something), otherwise not. Recognition is good if it provides an optimal return (see, for example, the discourse on 'recognition as a management tool' and 'appreciative inquiry', in which positive relationships are developed with employees with a view to improving their performance), otherwise it is not. Subjectivism and instrumentalisation are, therefore, interlinked. They are two sides of the same coin. Nowadays, it is a commonly held view that it is not possible to discuss our goals in life rationally (as they are subjective), we can only promote means (including psychological techniques) to help the individual achieve their goals. In *Stand Firm*, I focused on the coaching industry as a symptom of this. Here, 'the customer is always right' and the coach, as a neutral mirror, is supposed to help the customer achieve self-realisation – but without any rational discussion of the legitimacy of their goals. If this is a fair reflection of the nature of coaching, then it is nothing more than unadulterated, subjectivist instrumentalisation.

Conversely, to take Aristotle seriously means insisting that there are ends, values and meanings that are defined by something that transcends the individual's subjectivity (and the whole 'what's in it for me?' question). For Aristotle, the basis of meaning is human nature itself. Some ways of living are more correct than others because they take greater cognisance of human nature. Critics will say that this is an example of the 'naturalistic fallacy' – that is, jumping from 'is' (factual sentences) to 'ought' (normative sentences) – and that it is logically invalid. However, using Aristotle's anti-instrumentalist approach, the answer to that objection is that, when talking about things with a purpose or function (be it hearts, knives, watches or people), it is possible to move from 'is' to 'ought' sentences, because by necessity every 'is' for these things already has a built-in 'ought'. From the sentences 'he is a teacher' and 'she is a doctor', we may conclude that 'he ought to do what a teacher ought to do' and that 'she ought to do what a doctor ought to do', precisely because the function (of a teacher or doctor) is defined by its purpose. We can only understand what a teacher or doctor actually *is*, if we understand what they do when they carry out their activities *well* (that is, when we keep in mind the 'ought' that defines their activities). We can also only understand what a heart *is*, when we understand what it *ought* to do in order to perform its function adequately (i.e. pump blood around the body).

Aristotle insisted that part of being *human* is to have a purpose (namely, to live in accordance with reason) – at any rate, we can say that many of the roles and positions that we adopt throughout our lives are predicated on a series of normative 'oughts' that define them. The specifics of these 'oughts' can be discussed and refined, but it does not make sense to say that what a teacher or a doctor *ought* to do is entirely subjective. If we accept Aristotle's thinking up to this point, then we are already well on the way to overcoming subjectivism and, therefore, instrumentalisation. There are limits to what teachers and doctors (and other similar roles) can be required to do, purely instrumentally, in order to continue to be defined – and for them to define themselves – as teachers and doctors. We can interpret the opposition to reforms and cuts in various professions in recent years in this light. For example, an academic might say 'If *that* is how you want us to run the university, then it is no longer a university, but a sausage factory, where you just calculate an "output" quantitatively, with no concern for the intrinsic value of science!' Or a teacher might say 'If *that* is the way you want us to run the school, then it is no longer a school, which rears children to be competent, democratic citizens, but a training camp for soldiers in the service of the competition state!' Or 'If *that* is what you call "modern general education", then the commercialisation of our schools is complete and we are no longer capable of providing a general education!' That which on the surface may look like a reactionary resistance to change can also be interpreted as a rational defence of the uniqueness and meaning of things.

All of this makes Aristotle's idea of the useless an empowering first line of defence against instrumentalisation: the useless is something we do, not to achieve something else, but for its own sake. It is an existential standpoint upon which we must be able to stand firm. We should not feel guilty about spending time on such useless activities, because, in an instrumentalised era, these are precisely the activities that offer the prospect of a meaningful life. Uselessness is the highest good. We should practise saying this to ourselves – not as an unthinking mantra, but as a constant reminder that what constitutes the most important thing in life is not up to me as a subjective individual, nor is it up to the agencies in society that seek to promote instrumentalisation.[5] Rather, some things are good because they are ends in themselves, and together we can protect them and make the idea of what constitutes 'the good' one of our existential standpoints in life on which to stand firm. What is good is not good because of what I get out of it (because it makes me healthy or happy, for example), or because I like it. On the contrary, I ought to learn to like 'the good' precisely because it is good, and teach my children to do the same. This provides an overall existential standpoint upon which to stand firm throughout our lives. But at this stage of the book, this standpoint is somewhat lacking in tangible content. What *is* it that is good and has intrinsic value? What *is* worth standing firm on because it is good *per se*? The chapters that follow will add flesh to the bare bones of these questions.

2

Dignity

Everything has either a price or dignity.

Immanuel Kant (1724–1804)

When the blockbuster *Titanic* premiered in 1997, I was one of the many who flocked to the cinema. It is a big film in every sense. A giant ship sinks. Love, hate and human destinies are literally shipwrecked. But one image in particular stands out in my memory. Bearing in mind that I have not seen the film again, and that psychological research shows how notoriously unreliable human memory is – especially as far as this kind of detail is concerned – it is entirely possible that my recall is not perfect. But that is not so important in this context. The image in question is from a scene in which it has become clear that the ship is going down. The passengers begin to panic. Some throw themselves overboard, others almost trample fellow passengers underfoot in their attempts to flee. Meanwhile, an elderly couple remain in their cabin, where they quietly and calmly lay down on the bed, embrace each other lovingly, and await their death. Confronted with the inevitability of what is about to happen, they face it with something resembling stoic peace of mind. I am probably embellishing the sentimentality of the scene, but I seem to recall a faint smile on their lips and an air of peace in the midst of all the tumult and panic.

The couple display what might be called dignity. They will not 'get anything out of' their calm, dignified reaction. Their response has no instrumental value, but nevertheless radiates a fundamental humanity that is both moving and inspiring. How would I react in a similar situation? I think about that quite often, as I sit, mildly afflicted by fear of flying, in an aeroplane buffeted by turbulence. What if the plane were suddenly to plunge earthwards and I only had seconds to live? Would I pass them in a dignified manner or would I scream and shout?

I do not think any of us know the answer for sure. Fortunately, very few of us will ever find out. However, from a psychological perspective, it is interesting that we are able to understand the significance and value of dignity at all. Why not just hurl ourselves to the floor and bawl away, we might ask? After all, we are about to die anyway... Indeed, and I would hasten to add that nobody has any right to condemn people who do lose it in such situations. Perhaps I would, too. But that is not the important point here. What is important is that we instinctively understand the value of the dignified response, despite the fact that it triggers no instrumental reward. Nothing comes of it except a moment of calm, which is an integral part of dignity itself. In a metaphorical and existential sense, we are all sitting in a plane that is plummeting to the ground. It probably – hopefully – will not hit the ground any time soon, but in principle it could happen at any time. We know for sure that we *will* hit the ground, just not *when*. In other words, we are mortal beings. Life is fragile, dependent on a muscle in our chest continuing to work – which it could theoretically cease doing at any moment. As the Norwegian writer Karl Ove Knausgård put it in the unostentatious opening lines of his mammoth work *A Death in the Family*: 'For the heart, life is simple: It beats for as long as it can. Then it stops.'[1] How are we meant to live with this knowledge? Shrieking, screaming and bawling our eyes out? Or with quiet dignity?

To my mind, the elderly couple in *Titanic* definitely displayed dignity, and it was dignity in a specific sense. Harking back to Aristotle and his philosophy of the virtues, we might call it dignity as a virtue – dignity in the sense of the ability to act in a dignified manner. The notion of dignity as a virtue is seldom discussed these days. While there is no shortage of books about how to be passionate, authentic, innovative or self-optimising, I know of no self-help book that focuses on dignity and helps us achieve it. Is there, perhaps, something inherently undignified in the prevailing worship of the self, which means that writing about dignity as a virtue is not an obvious choice? Aristotle would undoubtedly understand the *Titanic* example and approve of the couple's response to their inevitable fate. The later Stoics would certainly have understood it. Taking inspiration from Aristotle, they stressed dignified peace of mind as a fundamental value for human beings.

However, the concept of dignity is also referred to in a different, albeit related way – namely as an inherent aspect of human life. This is not dignity as a virtue, i.e. something that we possess to a greater or lesser extent, but what we might call dignity as an ontological principle – in other words, dignity as an integral element of humanity. Aristotle and the other ancient Greek philosophers did not have a concept for this. For them, there was nothing particularly dignified about being human, and life itself was not sacred. In historical terms, life only became sacred with the advent of monotheism. This principle was resurrected in the humanist thinking that emerged from the Renaissance. Prominent examples include the book *De dignitate et excellentia hominis* (On the Dignity and Excellence of Man, 1452) by the early Renaissance humanist Giannozzo Manetti, and Giovanni Pico della Mirandola's famous work *Oratio de hominis dignitate* (Oration on the Dignity of Man, 1486). The early humanists argued that a form of dignity is intrinsic to being human. If there is one thing on which it is worth standing firm in our instrumentalist age, it is this idea of elementary human dignity. One philosopher who, more than any other, made this a cornerstone of his thinking – even explicitly challenging instrumentalism – was the German Enlightenment thinker Immanuel Kant. Kant was an advocate of the second anti-instrumentalist standpoint presented in this book: dignity.

Value or dignity?

While Plato and Aristotle have had the greatest impact on the history of philosophy, I would put Kant in third place. In his three major – and difficult – works on pure reason (knowledge), practical reason (morals) and judgement (including aesthetics), he posed the fundamental philosophical questions: What can I know? What should I do? What can I hope for? Kant's life was notable only for its extreme lack of incident and drama. He lived all his life in Königsberg and was a bit of a slave to routine. Only twice did he deviate from his fixed daily pattern of intellectual work and walks: at the outbreak of the French Revolution (which meant spending more time reading newspapers), and when he read Jean-Jacques Rousseau's (1712–78) *Émile* (on education), which he was unable to put down.

In one of his shortest and most accessible books, *Fundamental Principles of the Metaphysics of Morals*, Kant wrote: 'In the kingdom of ends everything has either *value* or *dignity*. Whatever has a value can be replaced by something else which is *equivalent*; whatever, on the other hand, is above all value, and therefore admits of no equivalent, has a dignity.'[2] In the Prologue, I described how money acts like a set of scales – this is what Kant refers to as equivalence. Equivalence literally means 'of equal value', and money is used to measure and compare the value of otherwise completely different things. In monetary terms, Shakespeare's collected works (currently available for around £30) have the same value as a pair of cheap trainers. It is absurd to compare the works of the Bard with trainers, but the instrument we call money makes it possible to do so. And as we go about our day-to-day lives, we do not even notice the absurdity of this.

The 'kingdom of ends' that Kant describes is a community of rational beings – a community of the dignified. It is an ideal kingdom – we rarely inhabit it in practice, because we are not always rational and we rarely treat each other as ends in themselves. But we *can* see the world in that light – as populated by people who are ends in themselves – and we *can* try, as much as possible, to live in a way that fulfils the ideal of the kingdom of ends. Indeed, according to Kant, we have a duty to try, an endeavour that provides us with a significant existential standpoint, in the sense described in this book.

Often, we do not view the world in the light of Kant's idea of the kingdom of ends. For example, from a scientific perspective, the world consists of processes described by the laws of nature, but there is no end, meaning or value. From this perspective, the world is simply a complex machine, with no meaning other than that with which we endow it. This is the worldview perpetuated by Woody Allen when he asserts that life has no meaning. As noted in the previous chapter, Aristotle saw things completely differently. For him, the world itself had purpose and meaning. However, modern science, from Galileo and Newton onward – the science to which Kant relates – leaves no room for this. Kant attempts to point out that we, as human beings, cannot just live in a mechanical world of cause and effect, but must also relate to what he calls the kingdom of ends. Some readers might object to this, and argue that our lives are necessarily determined as part of the processes of nature – we are not free and therefore we have no special dignity. Kant would respond that nobody knows if this is true, but we know that we cannot *live* under the assumption that everything in our lives is determined. From an existential perspective, we must presuppose that we have freedom and dignity, because otherwise life has no meaning (see more on this in Chapter 9 on freedom). And we can *think* freedom, which according to Kant is enough, because it means that we are able to relate to each other in this light – in the light of the idea of the kingdom of ends. Or, as William James put it: 'My first act of free will shall be to believe in free will' (see the Prologue).

As Kant says, 'In the kingdom of ends everything has either value or dignity.' People buy and sell things from and to each other, and in doing so put a price on all sorts of goods and services. However, when we exchange them with each other (and render them equivalent by means of money) they only have a price and no dignity. The quote above continues as follows (and forgive me for quoting a few more lines of Kant's somewhat convoluted language):

> Whatever has reference to the general inclinations and wants of mankind has a market value; whatever, without presupposing a want, corresponds to a certain taste, that is to a satisfaction in the mere purposeless play of our faculties, has a fancy value; but that which constitutes the condition under which alone anything can be an end in itself, this has not merely a relative worth, i.e., value, but an intrinsic worth, that is, dignity.

Let me try to explain. According to Kant, food, shelter and clothing, i.e. things that meet our basic needs, have a market price. So too do skill and diligence, which are also bought and sold in the labour market. Our abilities and skills – or competencies, as they are called nowadays – all have a relative value, but are not valuable *per se*. The same is true of our wishes, preferences and tastes, which are formed through life, including under the influence of advertising and fashion, in a thoroughly commercialised consumer society. These things have what Kant calls a 'fancy value'. Kant also mentions 'lively imagination and humour', which have increased in fancy value since his day. Indeed, they are often a prerequisite in many modern job ads (though more often expressed in terms such as innovation, passion, dedication and sense of humour). However, both – that which has market value and that which has fancy value – are purely instrumental and have no intrinsic value. The only things that do have intrinsic value are those which are an end in themselves, i.e. *people* – the subjects of the kingdom of ends – and that which people do, which is connected to their status as members of this kingdom. Following the passage quoted above, Kant goes on to use the terms 'fidelity to promises' and 'benevolence from principle'. These phenomena, like people, have no value, but they do have dignity. We cannot buy, sell or assign a value to 'fidelity to promises' (honesty) and 'benevolence from principle' (goodwill). If we do that, we will have 'bought' the phenomena ('I'll give you £100 if you promise to say nothing'), thus making them relative to the price paid for them, which robs them of their dignity. Honesty and goodwill are phenomena with intrinsic value. We might express this in a paradoxical manner: the only things with true value are those upon which we cannot put a price.

Kant would insist that human beings have a form of intrinsic value. Our main distinguishing feature is that we possess dignity – because, according to Kant, we have autonomy. This literally means that we are self-legislating. Not in the sense that each of us can, quite subjectively, decide what is right and wrong. Rather, the opposite: because we are rational beings, we are in a position to determine what is right and wrong *in general*, completely independently of our subjective wishes and preferences. It is not our 'vision' or our 'gut feelings' that determine what is right or what our duty is in life. Indeed, there are things that we have a duty to do, whatever we may think or feel about them. Above all, we have a duty to respect and protect other people's dignity as human beings. We must not exploit them for our own gain, or treat them solely as means to be exploited for a particular end. Humankind has always been and always will be, at all times and in all places, an end in itself. As Kant writes, in his characteristically abstruse and formalistic manner: 'So act in regard to every rational being (thyself and others), that he may always have place in thy maxim as an end in himself.'[3] To be human is simply to be an end in yourself.

Of course, we cannot avoid *also* having instrumental relationships with other people. When we buy something, for example, the shop assistant is a means by which we are able to do so, just as the mechanic is a means to repairing a car. This is entirely legitimate, according to Kant. But we must *also* act as if these people are ends in themselves. We should not relate to others *only* as means, but always *also* as ends in themselves. We have a duty to do so because otherwise we belittle their status as people – as autonomous, rational beings. Quite simply, we must treat people as people, not as things.

Dignity today

Unfortunately, it is all too easy to find examples of people being treated solely as means and not as ends *per se*, of their human dignity being belittled by having a value attached to it. Slavery and human trafficking are the most extreme examples and are, sadly, still prevalent to this day. But we also find it, albeit in a far less extreme and morally reprehensible form, woven into the fabric of large parts of our culture. When the influential American life coach Tony Robbins preaches that 'Success is doing what you want to do, when you want, where you want, with whom you want, as much as you want', he is giving voice to a way of thinking in which the value of other human beings is made relative to the individual's own wishes. According to Robbins, success does not consist in seeing beyond your own desires and thinking of others, but in doing exactly what you want, even 'with whom you want'. To the extent that other people are even part of the equation, they are merely tools that the individual uses to achieve his or her own desires. If we subscribe to Kant's idea of human dignity, success cannot be defined in this way. Success must – in a moral sense – involve treating others as an end *per se*, and not just as a means to get what we want.

Unfortunately, assigning a value to people has also become widespread. In some countries (including Australia, New Zealand, Japan and Austria), the authorities operate a points system for immigrants. Someone with a PhD will usually have more points than someone with a bachelor's degree. Someone who speaks English will have more points than someone who speaks Chinese. Entry into the country is granted for those deemed to represent a net gain to society, measured according to various parameters for which they are allocated points. If they do not have enough points, they are unwelcome. This perspective does not see human beings as having intrinsic value, but as having value relative to external ends associated with the national economy. People are assigned a value in the form of points, but their dignity is not considered. In general, instrumentalisation in our modern societies often means that people become a resource used to serve a particular end – improving GDP, PISA rankings or competency audits – rather than an end in themselves. We casually refer to human resources and human-resource management, and have completely forgotten how fundamentally instrumentalist the term actually is. People are not resources on a par with oil or iron ore, to be exploited and optimised as much as possible. Rather, they are autonomous beings with a form of dignity and should never be reduced to a means, an instrument or a resource.

The question is, then, how do we revive Kant's humanistic idea of the fundamental dignity of humankind? The answer is probably that it would only be possible as a collective endeavour at a political level, by insisting that policy always treats citizens as people, not as economic resources or consumers of goods and public services. Until that happens, as ordinary people, we need to keep reminding ourselves that everybody has a basic dignity and deserves our respect. I hope that, in this sense, dignity will serve us well as one of our existential standpoints – both ontological dignity and dignity as a virtue that we endeavour to incorporate into the way we live our lives. Unfortunately, as mentioned previously, there is a severe lack of self-help literature and psychological research focusing on this form of dignity. Having spent many years studying psychology, and later researching and teaching the subject, I do not remember ever encountering the concept. Not once – which is pretty astonishing. This is probably because modern psychological culture struggles to come to terms with dignity, as it is impossible to instrumentalise or monetise it. It's a good thing, then, that we have the useless old philosophers to remind us of this important existential standpoint on which to stand firm.

3

The Promise

Man is an animal with the right to make promises.

Friedrich Nietzsche (1844–1900)

Although this book does not adopt a Nietzschean perspective, this chapter does consider in detail one of Friedrich Nietzsche's many profound observations about humankind. Nietzsche is one of the most controversial but also most misunderstood philosophers. A troubled figure, Nietzsche led a life wracked with illness, drama and tragedy, culminating in a mental breakdown in Turin in 1889, allegedly brought on by the sight of a horse being mistreated – a surprising reaction for a thinker who had inveighed against compassion. On balance, it is more probable that he actually collapsed in the street that day due to advanced stage syphilis.

I mentioned previously that some people consider Nietzsche a nihilist – in other words, a thinker who completely rejects meaning and value. In reality, Nietzsche saw nihilism as a threat that had to be overcome. A master of the aphorism, he is known for his pithy and irreverent analyses of the ancient philosophers, of whom he had in-depth knowledge through his studies as a classical philologist. He was interested in Greek art, culture and drama, but also science and Darwinism. Nietzschean philosophy is not a carefully constructed system of thought. He had a tendency to 'philosophise with a hammer', as he put it. In other words, he set about dismantling established truths by tracing their origins and reception history (most notably, in his analysis of what he called the Christian 'slave morality'). His approach was 'genealogical', a method of study continued in the twentieth century by the French philosopher Michel Foucault (1926–84), in particular. But Nietzsche was not merely genealogical in his thinking – not just out to provoke and expose the fact that the accidents of history shape our collective beliefs (especially moral ones). Some of his work, whether intentionally or not, is edifying – or at least I will attempt to paint it in this light by focusing on his discussion of the right to make promises. In fact, I would go as far as to name 'the promise' as a basic existential standpoint.

The significance of the promise

In the second essay of his polemic on the genealogy of morality (1887), Nietzsche asks: 'To breed an animal with the prerogative to promise – is that not precisely the paradoxical task which nature has set herself with regard to humankind? Is it not the real problem *of* humankind?'[1] Nietzsche answers his own question in the affirmative – for him, the fact that humans are capable of making promises is one of the keys to understanding humankind. According to Nietzsche, humans are animals driven by the same basic forces of nature as the antelope or lion, but they are differentiated by virtue of being able to make promises. As far as we know, no other animal has this attribute. Only humans have the reflexive self-consciousness and understanding of the link between today and tomorrow that are prerequisites for making promises. When we think about it, we realise that the fact that we are able to promise things to each other is absolutely fundamental to us as human beings. If we did not have the ability to make promises, then marriages or other long-term relationships based on fidelity (perhaps even 'till death do us part') would be impossible. Nor would it be possible to enter into agreements and contracts for goods or property ('I promise to pay tomorrow'). Day-to-day life could not function either, as it is based on the constant making of promises ('I'll do the dishes') – both big and small, explicit and implicit. No human community or society would be sustainable without our fundamental ability to make and keep promises.

The philosopher of language J.L. Austin (1911–60) even argued that merely making an observation about the world is, in a functional sense, the same as making a promise. Even when we say completely innocuous things like 'it's raining', we submit to an obligation to believe it (until we learn otherwise) and act upon it (e.g. take an umbrella with us). To make a promise entails declaring yourself willing to be held accountable for it. Similarly, the fact that we make statements about conditions in the world means that we are (at least implicitly and in principle) declaring ourselves willing to be held accountable for them.[2] When we say 'it's raining', or anything else, the statement also implies 'I promise you!'

In this sense, the promise is important, on an absolutely fundamental human level, as an expression of trust and credibility. Our ability to enter into lasting relationships with others, and our communication in general, is based on an implicit assumption that we will stick to our promises.

The promise and guilt

Humans are, of course, fallible. Sometimes we are unable to keep our promises. When we fail to do so, we ought to feel guilty. In psychological terms, guilt exists to tell us that we have done something wrong – such as broken a promise. It has long been popular to want to eliminate guilt from our lives. Self-help and personal development books frequently present guilt, shame and a bad conscience as things to be avoided. Granted, they can be problematic emotions, because people sometimes feel guilt and shame even if they have not done anything wrong, e.g. people who suffered abuse as children. In situations like those, it is important to realise that there is absolutely no reason to harbour these negative emotions. However, many of us have the opposite problem. We do *not* feel guilt, even when we have done something wrong. In situations like those, we may not even realise that we have done something wrong, precisely *because* we lack the sense of guilt. Guilt acts as a moral compass – without it, acting morally is difficult – so it is important that children learn to feel guilt when they *are* guilty (but not, of course, when they are innocent).

A sense of guilt can therefore be regarded as the glue that holds our morality together – in effect, it is the flipside of the broken promise, which is perhaps why we would not like to be without it, despite the fact that it can be extremely painful. In his 1973 novel *The Man Who Wanted to Be Guilty*,[3] Henrik Stangerup mounts a literary defence of the existential importance of guilt. The book is set in a dystopian society ruled by therapists, where people are valued, accepted and understood – even if, like the protagonist, they have murdered their spouse. The man tries to be found guilty, but guilt has no meaning in a society where people have been deprived of personal responsibility. Stangerup's analysis is no less relevant today, in our psychology-based and therapy-ridden culture, which emphasises positivity and recognition rather than guilt and shame in many spheres of our lives.

The contemporary philosopher Judith Butler has revived Nietzsche's thinking in an attempt to develop an understanding of humankind based on the ability to feel guilt and make promises.[4] Butler believes that it is essential to our concept of a human being (she talks about 'the subject') that people are capable of giving 'accounts' of what they get up to. Usually, people are able to justify their actions – at least to the extent that they have acquired language. According to Butler, it is primarily through moral relations that the subject is created, rather than the other way around, as is often asserted in our individualistic culture, i.e. that the subject chooses a morality once they are fully formed. According to Butler, this is erroneous, as there is no real subjectivity prior to or independent of morality, and there is no subjectivity prior to or independent of power (as Foucault also claimed). From this perspective, power and morality are two sides of the same coin. Morality exists because people have power over themselves and each other (and vice versa). Or, as Kant put it, a moral 'ought' presupposes a 'can' – i.e. the power to act in certain ways.

This may sound somewhat cryptic, but it is actually very simple. We start to exist as human beings when we are asked – or even forced – by others to account for our actions. We start to be able to relate to ourselves when others intervene in our lives and insist that we explain ourselves. If we are never asked to account for ourselves, we remain in a state of immediacy, unable to develop reflexive self-consciousness. Butler refers here to Nietzsche, who believed that the reflexive subject arises through, as he rather dramatically put it, 'fear and terror'. By this he means that we begin to account for our actions the moment we are asked to do so by someone in a position of authority (e.g. a parent or teacher) within a sanctioned system of law and punishment. A child encounters the requirement to account for themselves when they do something wrong or forbidden (e.g. when they spill a cup of milk), and their parent asks, angrily, 'Why on earth did you do that?' The child may not even know why, but they are still required to account for or justify their (unfortunate) behaviour. In this situation, the child is treated as a responsible being, even before becoming one in any formal sense. The magic of developmental psychology is that it is only with time that children *become* responsible beings (with the right to make promises, as Nietzsche puts it), and only because they have already been treated as such previously. In this context, guilt is extremely important. As Butler puts it, 'guilt makes it possible to be a subject'.[5] The accusation of guilt draws the child into a relationship in which they are more or less forced to evaluate themselves and their actions, as part of a process that determines their guilt or innocence. Nobody becomes a responsible being overnight or following a single accusation of guilt; rather, it is a process that takes years, during which we gradually cultivate our subjectivity, thereby creating a self-reflexive individual capable of accounting for itself. In other words, we become a being who has the right to make promises.

Instrumentalised promises?

We have established that there is an inherent link between the promise, morality, guilt and becoming a responsible adult. Humans take their first step towards becoming capable of action when they are asked (or forced) to account for themselves in relation to a set of norms with which they can break (for example, the norm of not spilling milk on the table). This process of accounting for themselves may involve either explaining that they were not responsible for what happened ('it wasn't deliberate'), which can lead to a form of regret on the part of the wrongdoers, or confirming their responsibility, which may lead to a genuine apology ('I did it. I'm sorry. Please forgive me'). The acting, reflexive human being is therefore formed in relation to a set of moral values – and specifically in relation to guilt, which is the *feeling* of morality. It is from this that we derive our fundamental ability to make promises and to be held accountable for them. The ability to accept or deny culpability (but at least to consider it) is the hallmark of a mature, self-reflexive human being.

Nietzsche's 'animal that makes promises' is a human being who is able to say: 'It was (or was not) my fault!' In a sense, this is the whole foundation of responsibility, morality and sociality in a human society.

However, in our instrumentalised culture, this foundation is in danger of being eroded. For example, what some call the 'project society' is based upon a new and more transient culture of agreements.[6] Increasingly, things are agreed *until further notice*. We promise each other things *for the time being*. After all, we might make a promise, only for something better to come along – an invitation to a better New Year's party, a better job, a better boyfriend. This is the perpetual dilemma faced by those who suffer from FOMO (fear of missing out). When promises are only *for the time being*, they are, strictly speaking, no longer promises. They are at best – but also at worst – instrumentalised promises that only benefit the person making them *for the time being*.

The act of promising somebody something is, in principle, unconditional. When we marry, we promise to stay together 'till death do us part'. Most couples are only too aware of the divorce rate and know that the odds against them being an exception are high – but they do not let empirical evidence get in the way of the promise to be faithful to each other. 'I promise to remain faithful to you unless something better comes along and I change my mind' just does not cut the mustard as a wedding vow. A promise *cannot* be instrumentalised without destroying the existentially significant nature of the promise. Promises are worth standing firm on. There is something elementary and dignified about keeping a promise, even if we get nothing from it other than sticking to what we agreed. In that sense, the promise is an existential standpoint – it cannot be instrumentalised, it has intrinsic value. If we do not strive to stand firm on our promises, we undermine the nature of humanity.

4

The Self

The self is a relation that relates to itself.

Søren Kierkegaard (1813–55)

Søren Kierkegaard is, without a shadow of a doubt, the most famous Danish philosopher. A master of theological, philosophical and literary dialogue, his writing consists of a complex maze of different voices and pseudonyms that still inspires analysis and interpretation. Many fine books have been written about his life and work, but here we will concentrate on one of his key existentialist ideas. The famous introduction to his book *The Sickness Unto Death* – written under the pseudonym Anti-Climacus, but published under the name S. Kierkegaard – reads:

> Man is spirit. But what is spirit? Spirit is the self. But what is the self? The self is a relation which relates itself to its own self, or it is that in the relation [which accounts for it] that the relation relates itself to its own self; the self is not the relation but [consists in the fact] that the relation relates itself to its own self.[1]

At first glance the quote may sound rather cryptic, but what Kierkegaard is saying is simpler than it seems.

61

Firstly, he defines humankind as spirit, and asks what exactly spirit is. His response – that spirit is the self – immediately leads to a new problem, i.e. defining the self. He determines that the self is a relation that relates to itself. In other words, the self is not an object or substance, it is a relation. But between what? The quote does not provide the answer, but Kierkegaard would have said that humankind is both a physical and mental being – a synthesis of body and soul. Nowadays, we would probably use the terms 'mental' and 'biological'. However, the mere fact of a relation between soul and body – the mental and the physiological – does not yet constitute a self in the Kierkegaardian sense. This relation only becomes spiritual, and thus a self, in the act of relating to itself. In other words, the self is neither our psyche nor our biological body, nor the sum of those parts, but the act of relating to the synthesis (or relation) between them. The self, therefore, consists of the fact that we not only relate to our psyche, body or the world in general, but that we are able to relate to *how* we relate to all of these things.

This may be easier for the modern, secular reader to understand if we replace the concept of the spirit with that of culture. The modified quote would then say that a human, as observed by itself, is a cultural being. Culture conveys a relation between nature (including the body) and the psychological. The concept of culture comes from its Latin root *cultura*, which means tilling or cultivating. Sometimes, culture is posited as the opposite of nature, but it is probably more accurate to say that culture is a *form of nature*, i.e. a cultivated form. Think of agriculture. Humans have *cultivated* plants and fields for millennia. It is still nature, but it is nature that we have processed. In this sense, no cultural products – e.g. art, language or social conventions – are unnatural. They are just ways in which nature has been cultivated or processed in order to mediate our relation to it. Culture consists of a mediated relation to the world. Correspondingly, to have a self is to have a mediated relation to yourself and the world. All animals eat, sleep and transfer their genes to the next generation, but human cultures mediate how these things are achieved. As a result, these activities take different forms in different parts of the world, due to different traditions regarding food, family structures and the rhythms of daily life.

We might also explain the human self and culture by saying that all living things exist in relation to the world: plants that move to catch the sun relate in a sense to light energy; the dog eating a sausage relates to both its own hunger and to the food. But neither plant nor dog have a self in the Kierkegaardian sense – neither is capable of relating to *how* they relate to the world. Just like every other living thing, humans relate to the world – but what makes us unique is the ability to relate to *how* we relate to the world. If we want a tan we can, like the plant, move with the sun, but we can also hide in the shadows, because we have read that exposure to sunlight increases the risk of skin cancer. No matter how strong our desire to bask in the sun, we can also relate reflexively to this desire based on (culturally determined) knowledge of its consequences. The plant cannot. Like the dog, we may also feel like eating a sausage, but we might also avoid eating meat, because we are vegetarian, we care about climate change or we are on a diet (in other words, we have culturally determined ideas about meat). The dog cannot be on a diet. Well, it could be, if its owner chose to impose one, but it cannot choose to go on a diet of its own free will. Why not? Because it is not able to relate reflexively to its own hunger. It may be hungry and search for food, but it is not capable of relating to whether or not it should act on its hunger. The dog undoubtedly has a temperament, and perhaps even a personality (some are more timid than others), but it does not have a self, and therefore it has no self-relation. This is also why we do not hold the dog morally responsible if, for example, it eats all of the sausages against its owner's wishes. We can get annoyed, shout at it and try to train it not to do it again (based on fear of our anger), but we cannot be morally indignant about its behaviour because it is not responsible for its misdeeds. Indignation is only legitimate if the other party is able to relate to its actions – i.e. if the party involved has a self in the Kierkegaardian sense (and thus belongs to what Kant called the kingdom of ends). Again, this touches on what defines 'the human' – and in a sense serves as the entire foundation for our ability to relate to the meaningful life – which makes it very definitely a standpoint on which it is worth standing firm.

The relation is constituted

In brief, Kierkegaard presents the self as a reflexive process. The self is not an object or a substance, but a process – something that *happens*, rather than something that *is*. It is a relation that relates to itself, and our ability to relate to ourselves is fundamental to being human. Without this ability, we would be like the other animals: driven by physical impulses or urges. When the dog is hungry, it looks for food, unless it senses a different and stronger impulse that drives it to do something else (for example, because it is afraid). However, while adult humans have impulses, we *also* relate reflexively to them and consider whether or not to act on them. This ability to reflect is not something that we created ourselves. Kierkegaard asserts this by pointing out that the self-relating relation that makes up the self is constituted by something *other* than that self. He would contend that this other is God – because for Kierkegaard, God created us as a self, i.e. as a spiritual being.

A secular interpretation, which ties in with developmental psychology, would be that it is our society or culture – the others – who constitute the self. We do not become reflective selves in an isolated process of self-development, but because we relate to ourselves through other people. In order for the small biological blobs that are new-born humans to become self-relating selves – and in that sense, become individuals with Kantian dignity – they must see themselves through the eyes of others. We only learn to relate to ourselves because others have first related to us. In this sense, we owe ourselves, literally, to others. We saw this in the previous chapter, on the development of guilt and responsibility.

This is an early twentieth-century psychological concept that was formulated, almost in parallel, by the social psychologist George Herbert Mead (1863–1931) in the United States and Lev Vygotsky (1896–1934) in the then Soviet Union, among others. In the Prologue, I was fairly critical of psychology, but this is an important phenomenon that the science of psychology has described in great depth. In the wake of Mead and Vygotsky, modern developmental psychology has analysed in depth how humans develop in interpersonal relations, including how they gradually adopt other people's perspectives as their own, and in this way become their selves 'from the outside', based on the balanced reactions of those who care for them. The self is always developed via others. Our reflexive self-relation – or simply the self, in the Kierkegaardian sense – is the result of social relations. Vygotsky clearly illustrates this in his famous analysis. He says that a child's innate biological tendencies are transformed into reflexive acts of will when adults – especially the parents – interpret the child's behaviour. For example, the toddler has an innate grasping reflex and will instinctively reach out to appealing, colourful and moving objects in their field of vision. This is not something the child has learned – in that sense, it is a natural act. Sometimes, however, the child will reach for an item beyond its grasp, and a more capable adult will have to step in and hand it over. The adult interprets the child's instinctive grasping reflex, which points at an object that the child wants to get hold of, and therefore the toddler gradually learns that they can direct the adult's attention by pointing. What starts as pure reflex (grasping) becomes a deliberate act (pointing). This only happens because adults interpret the pointing *as if* it is deliberate *before* it becomes deliberate, which means that the child's action gradually *becomes* real pointing. This key moment in the magic that is developmental psychology happens in the 'zone of proximal development'. The adult is always well ahead of the child in terms of development, and helps it gradually acquire the skills to do things that at first they are only able to accomplish with grown-up help.[2] Only in this way, and within a cultural context, does the self develop as a self-relating relation. However, things can go wrong if the adult gives the child too much responsibility and over-estimates their capabilities – e.g. when 'child-centred learning', an idea that has long been widespread in the educational world, is taken too far. Another potential problem is if the adults are 'helicopter parents' and do not allow the child to have any responsibility of their own. The zone of proximal development consists of a balance between these extremes, and requires that the adult understands the child's situation. It is in social situations that the child's behaviour is interpreted as consisting of meaningful, deliberate actions, which in turn allow them to gradually acquire the relevant skills. This corresponds with Butler's point from the previous chapter: that the child develops a sense of responsibility by being held accountable (to an appropriate extent).

Moral self-relation

At first glance, there is a gulf between a Danish Protestant theologian like Kierkegaard and a Russian Marxist-oriented psychologist like Vygotsky. And indeed, I focus solely on one key shared aspect of their thinking: that the self is a reflexive process determined by something other than ourselves – for Kierkegaard, by God; for Vygotsky (and his American counterpart Mead), by the social community. At this stage, the reader may be wondering why I have nominated the self (as a self-relating relation) as an existential standpoint on which to stand firm, since in the Prologue I criticised our age for worshipping the self as a deity and making it the centre of life. I stand by that critique. There is no contradiction, because I am referring to two very different notions of the self. The self that is determined by a community and is capable of becoming a relation that relates to itself is a totally different kind of self than the one promulgated in the vast majority of self-help literature, where the self is usually considered to be an inner, individual truth or core to be set free. When we talk about 'self-realisation', the self in question is usually one that is already there. However, this is not the case in the Kierkegaardian developmental-psychology interpretation, where the concept of *formation* (rearing and educating) is more relevant. The self is not something that is *realised*, but must be *formed* in relation to something other than itself – namely the historical traditions for human co-existence that structure our interactions, and from which the child derives experiences from the very beginning of their life. As we have seen, we always understand ourselves via something *other* than ourselves (other people's expressions and reactions), and not, for example, by isolating ourselves from the world and being purely introspective. We are only something because of our relations with others. The self is the name given to the ability to relate to these relations. Kierkegaard is often described as an individualist thinker, but that is only partly true, because his basic concept of the self requires an agent outside of the individual in order to determine or form the self. More recent research describes him as a social-psychology-oriented thinker.[3]

In a Kierkegaardian sense, the self and the self-relation can also be interpreted as consisting of an ethical or moral process (I use these terms synonymously here).

The fact that we are capable, unlike non-human animals, of reflexively deciding whether or not to respond to our impulses (precisely *because* we are selves!) makes it a moral process. The philosopher Charles Taylor, in particular, advocates this.[4] He is very much in line with Kierkegaard when he points out that, as humans, we have the ability to consider our actions not only in the light of what we most desire (like animals), but also in the light of the moral value of our actions. We may, for example, want to ignore an appeal to support the victims of a natural disaster (perhaps due to meanness), yet at the same time think that this response is of lower moral worth than the desire to donate money. Having a reflexive self therefore enables us not only to have desires and wishes, but to have desires and wishes to have certain (other) desires and wishes for moral reasons. Taylor calls these 'second order desires' (that is, the desire to have certain desires). He calls the ability to assess options morally 'strong evaluations', whereas 'weak evaluations' are just about what we most want to do. People are defined as moral beings because we can relate to our wishes in the light of values that originate from something other than ourselves and our own desires. This is precisely why values can be moral.

The existential standpoints emphasised in this book may in themselves be considered moral values (especially perhaps the promise, responsibility, truth, love and forgiveness). People can relate to themselves via these moral values. Unlike contemporary subjectivism, I consider these phenomena real – they exist in our world, and form part of the reality that people experience. The self is the name for our ability to relate to ourselves via these phenomena or standpoints. This version of the self

– as a morally determined self-relation – is quite different to the prevailing concept of the self in our modern age. It is no surprise that even the concept of the self has now been instrumentalised. It has become a commodity to be optimised via various forms of self-development, to enable the individual to be successful at work and in their love life. We are not supposed to relate to ourselves because doing so is existentially meaningful, and in that sense is an end in itself, but because it may make us happy and successful. The self has become another 'tool' in the individual's pursuit of better performance. As one management guru after another will tell you, 'Your most important management tool is yourself!'

Kierkegaard's emphasis on the self as a reflexive relation determined by something other than the self (in my secular psychological interpretation, the community), combined with Taylor's emphasis on the moral significance of this self-relation, provides us with a strong defence against the instrumentalisation of the self. The self, in the Kierkegaardian sense, is not a thing, nor should it be made into a tool or commodity. The self is not a resource to be optimised, or to be monetised by human-resource managers. We cannot put a value on the self – it has dignity, but not a value. To insist on the importance of being a relation that relates to itself is something that has intrinsic value in human life. Without reflexive self-relation, there is no responsibility, no duty and no morality.

5

The Truth

Even if there is no truth, man can be truthful.

Hannah Arendt (1906–75)

The absence of women from the philosophical canon is scandalous, but nonetheless a fact. Until the twentieth century, hardly any women featured in the history of philosophy. The few exceptions (e.g. Mary Wollstonecraft in the eighteenth century) were known primarily for their thinking on women's rights. Fortunately, many leading philosophers are now women. I mentioned Judith Butler earlier in the book, and later we will hear about Iris Murdoch. However, one of the twentieth century's most important philosophers of all was also a woman: Hannah Arendt. Born into a (liberal) Jewish family in Hanover, she lived a rather dramatic life for an intellectual. She studied under Martin Heidegger (1889–1976), who later became a Nazi – although this did not prevent Arendt from having a long-term affair with him, for which she was heavily criticised later. After Hitler came to power in 1933, she was involved in helping Jewish children reach Palestine, but she had to flee to France

71

and was interned in a camp in the Pyrenees in 1940. She escaped along with another famous philosopher, Walter Benjamin (1892–1940). Unlike Benjamin – who tragically committed suicide, possibly to avoid being captured by the Nazis – Arendt made it to New York, via Spain and Portugal.

In New York, Arendt began to apply philosophy to major social questions. Her writings included works on the rise of totalitarianism and revolution. She is probably best known for her book on the trial of Adolf Eichmann, one of the architects of the Holocaust, who was brought to book in Israel in 1961, sentenced to death and executed. Arendt covered the first trial for *The New Yorker* and later described Eichmann's crimes as an embodiment of the 'banality of evil'. She did not mean, of course, that the crimes themselves were banal, but that his personality was unsettling in its ordinariness. There was nothing diabolical about Eichmann, who – without any apparent sense of morality – appeared to think that he had simply done his duty as a citizen of the German Reich. He was not driven by sadism, but by mere obedience. Perhaps Arendt's most influential idea is her concept of 'natality' – the fact that we, as humans, are born and give birth. It was in natality that Arendt saw the potential for hope and belief in the creative power of human action – something of a contrast to the dominant Marxist theories of the day. From this perspective, humans are not solely determined by external structures, but continually develop in unexpected ways, which means we have the capacity to act freely.

Arendt's 1958 book *The Human Condition* is a gem for anyone looking to identify existential standpoints. It focuses on what she calls the *vita activa* (active life). It outlines a famous distinction between *labour* (linked to the provision of basic biological needs), *work* (the creation of technology and cultural products) and *action*, through which humans, in one way or another, submit to the world. Like Aristotle, Arendt considers an action to be a practice 'that discharges its full meaning in the actual doing of it'.[1] In other words, a real action is its own end. According to Arendt, when we look at the interconnected web of actions that constitute a meaningful human life, we perceive life as *bios* rather than *zoe*, rehabilitating a distinction from classical Greek philosophy. *Zoe* (the root of zoology) refers to being in terms of species – be it human, canine, feline, etc. However, humans should not be understood exclusively in zoological terms, because our lives also have stories, in which our role is to *live* our life in a meaningful way – this is life as *bios* (cf. the concept of the *biography*).

The truth in an uncertain world

Arendt's thinking reflects the major political upheavals of the twentieth century. It is a world in which, and for which, as Arendt puts it, we must 'think without a banister' – i.e. the conditions for life and for thought are constantly undergoing change. How do we derive an existential standpoint from this? The following quote from *The Human Condition* puts it beautifully: 'even if there is no truth, man can be truthful, and even if there is no reliable certainty, man can be reliable'.[2]

The context for the quote is Arendt's discussion of Descartes (1598–1650) and the transition from the Middle Ages to a more enlightened era based on scientific methodology and reason. Arendt did not think that truth and reliability are present in the world as such, but that it is up to humans to bring these phenomena into the world through *our* truthfulness and reliability. Why? Why is it good to tell the truth and act reliably? If we ask about the utilitarian value of these existential phenomena, we run the risk of distorting them. Considered purely as actions, they are an end in themselves, and therefore have a kind of intrinsic value. Centuries earlier, the Stoic, philosopher and emperor Marcus Aurelius (121–180 BCE) had expressed the same thought: 'Although everything happens at random, don't you, too, act at random.'[3]

The realisation that we live in an unstable and changing world is important – and the sense that the world is transient has presumably only intensified since Descartes. We know now about the Big Bang, palaeontology, geology and Darwinian evolution, according to which even mountain ranges and animal species are constantly changing. Again, the mind is drawn to Woody Allen's depressing analysis of the lack of meaning. In philosophical terms, the recognition of the world's fundamentally random and ever-changing nature is called contingency. The world is contingent in the sense that things have been and will be different. Does this mean that it is naive to insist on an existential standpoint for meaning? No. Arendt and the other thinkers cited in this book would reply that it is more a matter of how we respond to contingency. In recent years, it has been popular to respond by saying that when we live in an unpredictable world, we must be flexible and adaptable. But this effectively means perpetuating a state of affairs rather than registering it and seeking to respond intelligently to it. A wiser response would instead be to say that because stability is not a *given* in the world, it is up to us to create it. We can stabilise a contingent and fluid world by striving to speak truthfully and act reliably. We will never be able to establish an eternal and immutably fixed structure for the world, but we can realise some of the important ethical values in human relationships – and that is probably all that we can hope for. This presupposes that we think about life 'from the inside' and do not objectify it by distancing ourselves from the very life we wish to understand.

Based on a Darwinian view of the world, some thinkers espouse the opposite of truth and reliability. The lie is of particular interest to evolutionary psychology – a field that is in essence a generalised utilitarian psychology, because its basic premise is that our beliefs and behaviour developed in order to facilitate the continuation of our genes. It is certainly difficult to imagine a society in which everyone always speaks the truth, as there are myriad conceivable circumstances in which a lie is considerate and ethically justifiable. But this is a long way from concluding that we often lie in a strategic manner in order to improve our social standing: 'Lies can help us climb the hierarchy, giving us an edge over others in the fight for funds, partners and prestige.'[4] There is a fine line between evolutionary psychology pointing out the adaptive function of the lie, and the outright legitimisation or even recommendation of lying as a strategy in life.

It may well be factually correct that, from an evolutionary perspective, lies can help us ascend the hierarchy and give us advantages in terms of power. But here we see how dangerous instrumentalisation is – the argument would be that we should not tell the truth because it has ethical value, but because it has utility value. Therefore, when the opposite proves to have utilitarian value – e.g. when the lie is seen as a way of gaining money, partners or prestige – it becomes acceptable to lie. I do not really believe that evolutionary psychologists think it is okay to lie about anything we like, whenever doing so might give us a slight advantage in social situations. However, by presenting it as a means by which to improve our lives, they are at least indirectly endorsing the lie. And why not? In the purely Darwinian world, there are no yardsticks other than that which has utility value.[5]

The dignity of truth

The truth Arendt refers to is an existential one. Or, at least, that is how I interpret it. It does not refer to scientific knowledge, but to the truth that emerges from the way in which we live our lives. In a world in constant flux, we can create islands of stability by telling the truth and acting reliably. These islands – families, institutions, organisations and nations – are only possible because people commit to recreating them constantly in a true and reliable manner. Here, Arendt is also talking about truth and reliability as requirements and as tasks that we encounter in our lives with each other. We could choose to turn our backs on them and just get on with life, celebrating eternal flexibility and adaptability. However, according to Arendt and other thinkers in this book, choosing truth, provided such a thing is possible, is more human and dignified. Inevitably, the requirement for truth will, from time to time, clash with other requirements. One of the great tragedies of life is that some dilemmas cannot be 'solved' in a mathematical manner.

Nevertheless, existential truth has a basic dignity that makes it an end in itself. We should not speak the truth in order to be healthy, successful or happy (although we may be lucky and achieve all three of these states at one and the same time). Rather, we should speak the truth and live reliably because it has value *per se*, because it is interlinked with us being able to live up to our commitments towards other people. That is why truth is an existential standpoint on which it is important to stand firm.

6

Responsibility

The individual never has anything to do with another person without holding something of this person's life in his hand.

K.E. Løgstrup (1905–81)

After Kierkegaard, K.E. Løgstrup is the most important and best-known Danish philosopher of all time. A professor of theology at Aarhus University, his writings covered a wide range of topics, including metaphysics, philosophy of life and ethics. The extent to which his thoughts are tied up with Christianity is open to debate. His best-known work, *The Ethical Demand* (1956), conveys a human or general ethics that is accessible to all, regardless of religious persuasion.[1] Løgstrup did not think that there was such a thing as a particularly Christian form of ethics. His philosophy was phenomenological – which literally means 'the science of phenomena' – and built on efforts to describe our experience of the world prior to developing theoretical knowledge of it. Theoretical knowledge of human ethics may include knowledge of how the brain functions, the evolution of co-operation and the selection of genes that predispose us to altruism. However, according to phenomenology, this theoretical knowledge is nevertheless knowledge of *something* – namely a phenomenon that exists in the world before humans start to theorise about it. Phenomenology aims to describe this basic pre-reflexive and pre-theoretical aspect of our life experience. This basic ethical phenomenon is the focal point of *The Ethical Demand*.

Løgstrup writes that 'the ethical life's basic phenomenon' consists of 'daring to venture forth and be met'.[2] This implies a demand that is not of the individual's invention, and which nobody, therefore, is in a position to revoke. We may try to ignore or even deliberately quash it, but the demand is still there. It is one of the basic foundations of life. As humans, we live in a state of what Løgstrup called interdependence – a reciprocal state of dependence and deliverance. In a broad sense, to venture forth means to turn to others. This requires trust, which Løgstrup, in his book *Opgør med Kierkegaard* (Confronting Kierkegaard), called 'sovereign manifestations of life' – because trust has a form of existential precedence over mistrust. Infants are delivered to the world and trust their guardians; only later do they learn to distrust. Adults, too, usually meet one another in a spirit of trust, which is why they are so easily fooled on *Candid Camera*, for example. We do not expect to be cheated, but trust that situations will generally be as they seem, and that other people are sincere.

We must constantly turn to others because our lives are interdependent. Hence, it is a basic fact of life that 'The individual never has anything to do with another person without holding something of this person's life in his hand.'[3] Based on this, Løgstrup deduces what he calls the ethical demand: 'The demand to take care of the other's life that is delivered to you.'[4] As he put it: 'From elementary dependence and immediate power, stem the demand to take care of the part of the other's life that is dependent on you, and which you have in your power.'[5]

The ethical demand consists of our fundamental responsibility to our fellow humans, a responsibility that stems from the fact that we have power over each other. Michel Foucault, the most prominent power theorist of the twentieth century, also believed that power is a ubiquitous phenomenon in interpersonal affairs. Løgstrup stresses that we can *never* interact with another person without wielding power over them. Despite the fact that his philosophy was in many ways quite different from Foucault's, both analyse power as a basic phenomenon of life, even as a productive phenomenon, as Foucault would put it, because it creates opportunities for action and demands. From Løgstrup's perspective, duty and responsibility arise from power. We have a duty to do something good, because it is in our power to do so. Power is therefore not necessarily something invidious or negative, to be eliminated in order to create 'power-free spaces', as has long been a popular aim in organisational contexts, e.g. when managers coach employees. According to certain contemporary management theories, it is conducive to staff development to temporarily suspend power relationships in the workplace in favour of openness, e.g. during performance and development reviews. However, for people who live in a state of interdependence, there is no such thing as a power-free space. Instead, there is a demand to wield power in the other's best interests and not your own.

This is the ethical demand, without which we would not be able to live the life that we do.

Where does the demand come from?

When I am teaching Løgstrup's ideas, the most common question asked by students is where the ethical demand comes from. In this day and age, we are more preoccupied with explaining than describing. We want scientific explanations of the origins of things. Løgstrup explores the demand by describing it in phenomenological terms, but offers no evolutionary psychology explanation for its origins. It may be debatable whether such an explanation is even possible, but that does not alter the fact that the demand exists. If we were forced to account for the origins of the demand, it is not possible to say much more than (as Løgstrup himself does) that it stems from our dependence on each other. The demand, which might also be called a responsibility or duty, stems from a natural fact about humankind. This natural fact has its own story, which may be recounted in evolutionary terms, about how humanity has evolved into a hyper-social species and that the lives of individuals are inevitably and closely interwoven. However, asking where the demand comes from as such is akin to asking about the origins of the validity of mathematics or logical operations. Who decided that two plus two equals four? Where does the fact that two plus two equals four come from? Nobody decided it. That is just the way it is, purely mathematically and logically. Who decided that when two hydrogen molecules bind to an oxygen molecule, we get water? Nobody decided it. That is just the way it is, purely chemically, when these basic elements interact. *The world* is like this, not just our perception of the world. Things exist that we did not create but which, in a manner of speaking, help create our lives – as we depend on logic, water and ethics. We might answer the question about the origins of the ethical demand in the same way. It *is* just the way it is that people who interact with each other are met with a demand to wield their power for the other's best interests. *The world* is like this, not just our perception of the world. We did not create this demand, but it is part of what creates us. However, unlike the chemical example, the ethical demand is not a mechanical, causal process (like molecules binding), but a *normative* demand (like logic). It is up to us, as human beings, to decide whether to try to comply with this demand or turn our back on it. No matter which option we choose, the demand is still there. We can deny responsibility for the other, but this does not diminish our responsibility – just as choosing to act irrationally does not diminish the validity of rationality.

A common objection to this is that ethics are perceived differently around the world. The ethical demand cannot, therefore, be universal. The answer to this is that, first of all, there is far less variation in basic perceptions of ethics than we might think. It goes without saying that we should not base our thinking about ethics on hugely deviant points of view, such as those of mass murderers like Anders Breivik, or twisted ideologies like that of Islamic State. All of the great religions and cultures do, however, have a great deal in common.[6] In most of the world, most people treat each other well most of the time. Unfortunately, we also have the potential to be malevolent, destructive and sadistic, but such actions are exceptions (even if they form the bulk of media content). We should not allow this to overshadow the extent to which ethical interactions are the norm in our day-to-day lives.

Secondly, even though specific intellectual means of referring to ethics may vary – which they do, of course – this does not alter the reality of the ethical demand. The demand was not adopted by a majority vote and cannot be abolished by any government. What varies between different cultures and eras is what Løgstrup called *moral* demands. He identifies a distinction between morality and ethics: 'From the radical ethical demand, no legal, moral or conventional regulation can be extrapolated. It is silent. . . . Justice, morality and convention are only prisms through which the ethical demand is spread, so right, morality and convention can be both indicative and misleading.'[7] Etymologically speaking, morality and ethics are not synonyms. Ethics is a Greek term, morality Latin. Many philosophers have distinguished between them precisely in order to highlight the difference between the universal and the variable. Løgstrup uses the concept of ethics to identify the one ethical demand that applies universally. Unlike the many varying moral demands (for good behaviour, politeness, etc.), the ethical demand is pre-cultural. It is a basic condition of life on which it is worth standing firm – because although it cannot be revoked, it can, unfortunately, be forgotten. And it is forgotten, quite easily, in our instrumentalised era, as our ethical lives are increasingly dominated by the question 'what's in it for me?'

For Løgstrup, it is quite clear that we do not act ethically because there is something in it for us. We act ethically because it is the right thing to do, quite independently of what we stand to gain or lose. In general, Løgstrup was sceptical about our tendency to focus on ourselves and our own needs. He criticised the dominant image of humanity, which disregards interdependence and considers human beings independent, strong and self-sufficient. He wrote, *inter alia*, 'Respect for each other's independence was used to make one's own self-formation legitimate, which is bound to end in a cult of the personality. The idea that led to this perception was that every human being was a world of its own, and the others were outside of it.'[8] We are not closed off, introverted worlds of our own. We 'face outward' towards the others who turn to us (and we to them). Nowadays, some educational researchers talk of self-formation as an ideal in an era when there is a lack of anything universal in relation to which we may educate ourselves. For Løgstrup, self-formation is a highly problematic concept – which, in his well-chosen words, easily leads to a cult of the personality. In our modern, fitness-focused selfie culture, it is all too easy to find examples of the self being cultivated in an almost cult-like manner. I think that Løgstrup would have felt extremely alienated in the world of today. Perhaps he would have said that it is tragic how quickly we have forgotten the necessity of there being something universal in relation to which to form ourselves – namely the ethical demand and the sovereign manifestations of life, which are not created or chosen by the individual, but are simply there as existential standpoints on which to stand firm in a life consisting of basic phenomena that are more constant than we might think.

Ethics of the hand

I will conclude this chapter by emphasising the epistemological potential of Løgstrup's metaphor of the hand. When he states that we always hold something of the other person's life in our *hand*, it is a well-chosen metaphor – because the hand says something about human beings as active participants, involved in the world. The hand brings us close to the world and to other people – we handle things and situations – and we experience the world through our physicality. We can, of course, also manipulate others (the word manipulation stems from the Latin *manipulus*, meaning handful), which is less admirable. Nevertheless, the hand is associated with a special understanding of humanity and ethics. Løgstrup sought to challenge the view that 'every human being is a world of its own'. In doing so, he clashed with the philosophy of consciousness, which has been dominant from Descartes in the seventeenth century via Kant to modern brain research, which claims that humankind is defined by consciousness, by its ability to observe and represent the world outside of the self. We used to think it was the soul that possessed these characteristics. Nowadays, they are attributed to the brain. But in both cases, knowledge is rendered quite passive, and we observe the world from a distance. This turns other people into objects, out there, among all of the other objects. The individual may be able to read meaning and significance into objects by virtue of the mind (soul or brain), but the world out there is in itself devoid of meaning and significance. Meaning is considered a subjective or mental property, one that does not exist out there in the world. This is the philosophical foundation for much of what I called 'passive nihilism' in the Prologue – the idea that meaning is inside us and that we must look inward to find it.

When Løgstrup writes that we hold something of the other's life in our *hand*, it is a reminder that the *other* is, in a radical sense, an acting and suffering being. The other is not my creation; I do not decide what the other needs. This stems from the relationship with the other and the ethical demand it implies. The hand is a metaphor for being in direct contact with the other, and not just with my *idea* of the other (i.e. as a subjective idea in my consciousness). In the next chapter, we will see that love may be said to stem from the difficult realisation that the other *is indeed* another – and not just a reflection of the self. By placing the hand at the centre of our relationship with the world – including with other people – Løgstrup identifies a certain immediacy in our lives. The classical philosophical conundrums about the reality of the external world and other people's consciousness are well-nigh incomprehensible if viewed from the perspective of our interaction with the world – including our 'handedness'. The conundrums emerge from the idea that we have somehow 'locked the human being into' its own consciousness or brain, and said that we do not know the world but only our experiences of it. But this is false. We *do* know the world directly, via our handling of it.

Another point about the metaphor of the hand is relevant in this context. The philosophical sociologist Richard Sennett has long been fascinated by craftsmanship as a historical practice that is, in many ways, under threat in an instrumentalised era, but he also highlights its potential as the basis for a broader ethical understanding. In his book on the craftsman as an existential and ethical ideal, he defines the craftsman on the basis of the desire to do something well for its own sake.[9] The craftsman – whether he or she is a surgeon, a carpenter, a programmer or a teacher – is preoccupied with what they do. Sennett operates with a very broad definition of craftsmanship, as a creative practice that has certain standards for good work, which newcomers to the trade must adopt and eventually learn to live up to. In most modern workplaces, however, it is usually assumed that people are motivated by money or by personal development, both of which are different from the job at hand – and in both cases, the activity becomes instrumental. There is nothing necessarily wrong with that, but Sennett believes that there is greater potential for meaning in the craftsman's desire to produce good workmanship for its own sake. Like Løgstrup, he believes that it is the acknowledgement of the other – that which lies outside and beyond the craftsman – that gives the activity content and meaning. Holding something of the other person's life in our hand places ethical demands on us. So does holding a well-crafted object in our hand. It reminds us that there is something that exists outside of us and to which we must respond in a certain way, based on standards for quality and good practice. Craftsmanship represents the human ability to be engaged in things – this presupposes that we venture forth, orient ourselves towards the other and open up to the world. To be engaged in the world, and in the other, is a fundamentally ethical ideal – it is this that Løgstrup describes as the ethical demand. It gives humankind an important existential standpoint on which to stand firm, one that cannot be instrumentalised without being destroyed.

7

Love

Love is the extremely difficult realisation that something other than oneself is real.

Iris Murdoch (1919–99)

Few philosophers write both wisely and beautifully. Iris Murdoch is one of them. She is one of my favourite philosophers. She wrote with precision and great insight on various philosophical and psychological themes, but is perhaps best known for her fiction, having written more than twenty-five novels between 1954 and 1995. She was also made into a household name by the film *Iris*, in which Kate Winslet played the young Murdoch and Judi Dench the older version. The film is not about her philosophy, at least not directly, but about her somewhat unconventional love affair with her husband of many years, John Bayley (Iris had many affairs, with both men and women) – and not least about her gradual deterioration due to Alzheimer's, which ultimately led to her death.

Murdoch was Irish, but studied philosophy at both Oxford and Cambridge before being made a fellow at Oxford in 1948. In the 1960s, she became a full-time author, but continued her philosophical writings. Her key work, *Metaphysics as a Guide to Morals*, was published in 1992. Early on, she wrote about the existentialist Jean-Paul Sartre (1905–80). Although she obviously respected him, she was highly critical of his existentialism. This is, in a sense, the *leitmotif* in her writing. For Murdoch, the problem with existentialism is that it portrays life as a series of choices that equip the individual with far too much power to assign meaning to things. Sartre divided the world into what he called *being-in-itself* (the naked and meaningless thing) on the one hand, and *being-for-itself* (human consciousness) on the other. One of Sartre's famous phrases is that existence precedes essence – it is the choice and the action that give form to life, and not vice versa. In Sartre's eyes, therefore, Proust is a great writer because he wrote brilliant works – he did not write brilliant works because he was a great writer. Consciousness is not something specific, but emerges from choices and actions. 'To exist' derives from the Latin for 'appear', and it is through consciousness of the subject's appearance that meaning, purpose and value come into the world. This makes existentialism a form of subjectivism, in which it is only the individual's choice of values that mean the subject has value at all. For Sartre, standpoints are therefore chosen or invented, while Murdoch believed that to a far greater extent they are given – something of which people can become aware and gradually discover. Central to Murdoch's thinking is therefore not *the choice*, but *the attention*. This also applies to her analysis of moral issues. She wrote that if we pay enough attention to what is going on around us, we will not have a moral choice, because what needs to be done will be self-evident.[1] Being a good person does not, in the first instance, consist of choosing this or that, but of paying attention – to others, to the world, to the actions that various situations call for – and not primarily to the self.

The sovereignty of good

Iris Murdoch was one of the few twentieth-century philosophers to hark back to Plato and ancient Greece. In Plato, she found a basic recognition of the reality beyond the subject and, not least, a celebration of a force for good – or 'the sovereignty of good' as she put it in the title of her most famous philosophical essay in 1967.[2] For Murdoch, good is a sovereign concept, as with regard to all other moral concepts we can ask the question 'but is it really good?' We should be just, yes – but is being just always good? This is a meaningful question because the requirement for justice may, for example, be incompatible with a demand to care for your loved ones. We should speak the truth – but is truth always good? This question, too, is meaningful because it is conceivable that, in many situations, lying could be a moral requirement. When we define good as something specific – an x – we must necessarily add that we mean a *good* x. It is not meaningful, on the other hand, to ask whether the good (thing) is good, because it is so purely by definition. According to Murdoch, then, for us as human beings there is necessarily something indefinable and partly incomprehensible about that which is good. Good has a reality that exceeds our limited comprehension. And yet we are able to recognise the good when we become aware of it in specific situations.

Murdoch was adept at articulating these situations. For example, in a famous philosophical fable, she tells of a mother-in-law who at first does not care for her daughter-in-law, because she finds the young woman unrefined and impolite. However, given her own good upbringing, she acts impeccably towards the young woman. Gradually, she comes to understand the daughter-in-law in a new way: as lively, spontaneous, funny and a really good partner for her son. There is no visible change in the mother-in-law – no change in her external actions or existential choices, as per Sartre. For Murdoch, the story is about the mother-in-law paying closer attention and liberating herself of her own prejudices and childish jealousy. The story revolves around the idea that it is not just a question of a subjective choice of perspective. According to Murdoch, there is a way to perceive the daughter-in-law that is more correct in a moral sense, as it is not obscured by subjective desires and motives. Once the mother-in-law starts to see the younger woman in a less prejudiced light and pays attention, she is better able to see the reality – for Murdoch, this is the most important moral virtue. In principle, Murdoch sees no difference between a scientific study and moral understanding. Both are a matter of paying closer attention to the world and moving beyond the individual's own subjectivity.

Examples like this enable us to understand good in glimpses, but we can never achieve a full theoretical understanding of what good consists of. If there were angels, writes Murdoch, they might be able to define good, but then mere humans would be unable to understand their definition. In this way, good becomes a metaphysical concept, similar to Plato's idea of the Sun in the famous Allegory of the Cave. Plato imagines people trapped in a cave, where the only reality they know consists of shadows cast on the wall by a fire. The shapes on the cave wall are merely a crude facsimile of the world outside the cave, which is illuminated and given life by scorching sunlight. However, where Plato talked of the good in allegorical terms, Murdoch's writings about humanity's relation to it are far more heavily based on experience. Whether or not we follow Murdoch's strong Platonic moral realism – the idea that good exists – it would be difficult, when we think about it, not to acknowledge her specific observation that we experience good as something that exists prior to and independently of the individual's will and experience. I cannot just decide for myself what counts as good. I cannot just choose what should be considered good. Rather, there is a kind of truth about what constitutes good and it transcends my subjective perspective. This is the essence of Murdoch's moral realism, which remained unpopular in philosophical circles until the late twentieth century, when it was taken up by prominent thinkers such as Charles Taylor and John McDowell. It is also possible to identify a connecting thread between Murdoch and Løgstrup, in terms of their moral outlook (in Løgstrup: ethics), as a demand that comes from outside and is not up to the individual to create.

Something other than yourself

Many of Murdoch's novels are about love, which is also a key theme in her philosophy. For this reason,

I decided to use Murdoch as a reminder that love – properly understood – is an existential standpoint that cannot be instrumentalised without being destroyed. Love was a fairly general concept for Murdoch. She described it as follows: 'Love is the perception of individuals. Love is the extremely difficult realisation that something other than oneself is real.'[3] Murdoch stresses the importance of perception (which, elsewhere, she usually calls attention) and of that which is something other than oneself. Attention and love are not only linked in relation to love, but also in relation to, for example, knowledge:

> If I am learning, for instance, Russian, I am confronted by an authoritative structure which commands my respect. The task is difficult and the goal is distant and perhaps never entirely attainable. My work is a progressive revelation of something which exists independently of me. Attention is rewarded by a knowledge of reality. Love of Russian leads me away from myself towards something alien to me, something which my consciousness cannot take over, swallow up, deny or make unreal.[4]

To be led away from one's self is essential for love – to let the other be the other on his or her own terms, as 'something which my consciousness cannot take over, swallow up, deny or make unreal'. Love is only possible if we accept the reality of a world outside ourselves – and that, Murdoch believed, requires honesty and humility.

Love between people is, of course, somewhat different to love of, for example, a language. Russian is not an individual, even if, linguistically speaking, it clearly has its own unique features. But human love is love between individuals. We love another as *another* and as *a whole* (in Latin, individual is synonymous with indivisible).

We do not love a random combination of characteristics that can be separated from each other. According to one professor of psychology, Jens Mammen, our sense of the concrete is what distinguishes us from animals (or from the other animals).[5] We know that there are unique single things and individuals that are moving through time and space. Two things or people that are qualitatively identical (e.g. monozygotic twins) are still different and unique, no matter how many qualities they may share (height, weight, personality traits, IQ, etc.). It may well be that somebody other than the one we love is stronger, thinner, smarter, taller, shorter, etc., but love is not based on such individual characteristics, nor on the sum of them.

Based on this understanding, there is something problematic in contemporary conceptions of love, as expressed, e.g. on dating sites, where the self is presented as a collection of more or less quantifiable properties. We seek a partner who meets a set of demands, but this reduces the other to the sum of his or her properties. Not only that, but these qualities can always be improved, and somebody else may well possess them in greater abundance. According to Murdoch, real love is reserved for that which cannot simply be replaced with something else. Permit me the indulgence of a slightly banal and sentimental example. In our home, we have an old rocking chair that is worn and the armrest constantly falls off. It is an heirloom with sentimental value. We could easily buy a new chair that – purely in terms of its properties – would be better. But it would not be the same chair. We love *this* chair (or at least my wife does) as a unique, irreplaceable single thing. We do not love the sum of its properties.

Love of self

These days, loving yourself has become something of a dogmatic maxim, as reflected in the countless self-help books entitled *Love Yourself* or some variation thereof. Typically, these books (like many others in the self-help genre) assume that it is good to accept yourself and not constantly be self-reproachful. However, in my opinion, applying the concept of love in this context, i.e. in relation to yourself, is problematic. Because if Murdoch is right, then we *cannot*, in the strict sense, love ourselves. To love means to be led away from the self and pay attention to another *as* another. To love involves, therefore, a forgetting of the self, whereby you give yourself to someone other than yourself. You cannot give yourself to yourself – this is as impossible as borrowing money from yourself. As understood by Murdoch, love simply presupposes a relation with another. This is also true of the erotic dimension of love. You can, of course, have sex with yourself, but an imagined other will often (perhaps always?) be present. Love, including in the sexual sense, requires that you are more than just yourself.

The Christian Bible says that we should love our neighbour as ourselves. If that is taken to mean the same as in the self-help books – where loving ourselves is a means by which to achieve happiness or improve our self-esteem so that others will love us – then I do not understand it. That sounds like an instrumentalised love: love the other *in order to* be loved yourself, and love yourself *so* others will love you. This makes love a something-for-something relationship, a kind of transaction, which is surely not the idea (at least not in the Bible). A common metaphor in the self-help world is the instruction given to airline passengers in the event that air pressure drops in the cabin and the oxygen masks drop down – put on your own mask first before helping the children. It is deployed as an example of the importance of helping (and loving) ourselves before we can help (and love) others. While it is certainly wise to follow this instruction in a depressurised aircraft cabin, I do not think that the situation adequately describes human love. At least not if there is anything to Murdoch's insistence that love is the recognition that *something else* other than oneself is real. The picture is also misleading in relation to what might be said to be the real problem we face today. In our modern era, many people have, metaphorically speaking, opted to stay in their seat and breathe into their oxygen mask (we call it mindfulness or self-development), but never wonder whether there are actually any pilots left in the cockpit or whether they have all fainted. We are all so preoccupied with helping ourselves that we ignore the larger structure of which we are a part, and the major social problems that threaten its development in general. To take an interest in this something greater (society and its problems) requires love in Murdoch's sense of the word. The quote used as the epigraph for this chapter continues: 'Love, and so art and morals, is the discovery of reality.'[6] Many people seem to be more concerned with discovering themselves than discovering reality. Or perhaps they think erroneously that the self *is* reality.

Today, many think that love is an emotion. What else would it be? As a result, we cultivate what the sociologist Anthony Giddens calls 'the pure relationship', which is only legitimate when it is based on (positive) emotions, and becomes illegitimate as soon as those feelings evaporate. Social elites have perhaps always had the privilege of basing their relationships on pure emotion. In his autobiography, the famous philosopher Bertrand Russell (1872–1970) relates the story of how, one day in 1901, he was out cycling when it suddenly struck him that he no longer loved his first wife (he married four times). So he rode home and informed her of this state of affairs, and that he wanted a divorce. Here, love is identified with a feeling – when it is gone, love is gone too. This is logical. But what if love is not a feeling? What if it is a *relation* to someone (or something) other than yourself, which may, naturally, give rise to all sorts of emotions: from infatuation and joy to anger and jealousy? In that case, if we identify love with a feeling, we will have based one of the most important things in life on a false concept. As Murdoch wrote, 'Love is the extremely difficult realisation that something other than oneself is real.' Characteristically, she uses the word *realisation* rather than, for example, *feeling*, because love cannot be identified by reference to a particular emotion or feeling. If that were the case, it would mean that we are not loved whenever this particular feeling is absent. Love, however, involves paying self-transcending attention to another.

Why does Murdoch describe the realisation that something other than oneself is real as 'extremely difficult'? Because now – as in 1959, when Murdoch wrote these words – we live in an increasingly self-absorbed era, in which many perfectly good words (trust, value, love) are at risk of being ruined by the relentless drive to prefix them with the word 'self'. Of course, it is not possible to direct self-transcending attention to another constantly. According to Murdoch, only angels are capable of that. But as an ideal, I believe that it is worth striving for. When love is a feeling, it fits in neatly with the general instrumentalisation of life that this book attempts to lay bare and criticise, because there is a risk of the other being deemed valuable only when they generate a particular positive feeling in us. The other becomes a tool for our own happiness. In his 1970 book on relationships, the influential psychologist Carl Rogers said that a relationship between people should only be maintained as long as there is what he called a 'reinforcing, growth-enhancing experience for each person'.[7] But what if the one we love is seriously ill? What if there is no guarantee that being with him or her will be 'reinforcing' and 'growth-enhancing'? Murdoch reminds us that love is not a feeling, but a radical form of attention to something other than ourselves. We should not, therefore, strive to love ourselves, because to do so would be a contradiction. Furthermore, love cannot be instrumentalised without ceasing to be love. 'I love you so that you love me' is a worthless statement. As Dan Baird of the Georgia Satellites sang in the hit of the same name, 'I love you, period.' Love must be unconditional, full stop, to prevent it from becoming part of the general wave of instrumentalisation.

8

Forgiveness

Forgiveness forgives only the unforgivable.

Jacques Derrida (1930–2004)

Jacques Derrida was an original and influential French philosopher, but is often viewed as an intellectual *enfant terrible*. By all accounts an extremely affable and generous person, his thinking was highly controversial and sparked countless intellectual disputes. In 1992, he was nominated for an honorary doctorate at the University of Cambridge, but several leading philosophers – both local and more far-flung – protested, calling him an intellectual charlatan, a mere provocateur, in the tradition of the absurd Dadaist art movement. The vote went his way, 336 to 204, but those who voted for him were mainly from literary and aesthetic subjects, while the philosophers voted against.

Why this hostility to a genial French philosopher? His thinking was often mischievous and deconstructive. Take, for example, his famous slogan '*il n'y a pas de hors-texte*' ('there is no outside-text', which is more often than not mistranslated as 'there is nothing outside the text'). The mistranslation is provocative because it seems to suggest that everything in the world is 'text'. In other words, that all phenomena – including physical, chemical and biological – are 'text' rather than material. The more correct translation avoids this misunderstanding, because it (far less radically) underlines that all 'text' (which here means all forms of meaningful content) only has meaning because it relates to other 'text'. A word like 'mother' has no meaning *per se* as a standalone linguistic expression – it only has meaning in relation to other words like 'father', 'child', 'woman', etc. Mapping out the relationships between expressions in order to capture their meaning was structuralism's big project.[1] Individual elements were believed to have meaning only within a larger structure, and text has meaning only within its context (literally 'with-text'). However, Derrida was one of the authors (perhaps even the main one) of the philosophical school known as post-structuralism, which abandoned the idea of a fixed structure that gives meaning. In his post-structuralism, words, phrases, signs and symbols have no fixed meaning. The meaning is 'forever deferred', as Derrida put it, in an endless chain of signifiers that refer to other signifiers (other text), without ever finding the real, authentic meaning. We can never, therefore, acquire ultimate insight into what a word, a phrase or a novel *actually – in reality* – means. This makes nihilism – mistrust of meaning *per se* – a perpetual threat to post-structuralism, and this is what provokes many of its critics. The term *deconstruction* refers to a (post-structuralist) literary theory and philosophical activity, designed to show that the meaning of things is not fixed and, where appropriate, suggest alternative meanings. By its very nature, deconstruction can never be completed, but is an eternally ongoing activity, which for Derrida was very much ethical and political. According to Simon Critchley, deconstruction can be understood as an ethical approach to reading that combats the narcissistic self-images and established truths of our era.[2]

Despite what many of his critics claimed, Derrida was no irresponsible or childish thinker just out to destroy everything for the fun of it. On the contrary, he was a highly ethical thinker – and one of the ideals that he stressed was that justice cannot be deconstructed. In a sense, this is his defence against nihilism. Even for the godfather of deconstruction, there are limits to what can be broken down and meticulously analysed. Nevertheless, there appears to be a gaping chasm between Derrida's project of breaking down our ideas about what is really real and Iris Murdoch's emphasis on the *other* – and the importance of human *attention* to it – in the previous chapter. Without wanting to belittle this chasm, I think that Derrida is often closer to other thinkers than his intellectual enemies would admit, for example to the work of Emmanuel Levinas (1906–95). Levinas might be considered a Jewish version of the Lutheran Løgstrup. They both focused on human ethical experience as something that arises from encounters with the other (which, in his peculiar metaphysical language, he called 'the face'). In this book, I allow myself to interpret Derrida as an existential thinker.

Love and the unforgivable

The previous chapter discussed love as a standpoint. Love and the need for forgiveness are often linked. As the old song goes, 'you always hurt the one you love'. And we can try to forgive those who hurt us, even if they do so out of (misunderstood) love. When people's lives are interwoven, there are always plenty of opportunities for them to hurt each other. This is where the question of forgiveness becomes important. Can everything be forgiven? Ought everything be forgiven? Extreme situations test the limits of forgiveness. The Danish film director Nils Malmros' latest (possibly last) film, *Sorg og glæde* (Sorrow and Joy), is about love in adult life. The story is centred on a tragic event in the director's life, when his wife, in a psychotic state and on a home visit from the psychiatric hospital, killed their nine-month-old daughter. The couple still live together today, decades later, in the very same house where the tragedy occurred. It is said that love conquers all – which Malmros can say with greater authority than most, 'because I know that it happens'.[3] Love conquers all, but it is thought-provoking that, at the same time, Malmros denies that the film is about forgiveness, although it has often been interpreted that way. 'Where there is no guilt, there is no need for forgiveness', he says.[4] Malmros has apparently always seen his wife as innocent and not herself when she committed the crime. Her illness meant she was not in control of her actions.

Nevertheless, we cannot help but ask ourselves how he – or we – would have reacted if mental illness had not played a part? Nobody knows, but it is difficult to imagine forgiveness being an option. There are, quite simply, some things that are unforgivable. Or are there? This is where Derrida comes in, with his surprising analysis of the phenomenon of forgiveness. Simply put, he contends that only the unforgivable can be forgiven – or, in his words 'forgiveness only forgives the unforgivable'.[5] The reason is quite simple: if something is forgivable, there is no reason to forgive it. Only the unforgivable requires forgiveness. Forgiveness is therefore only possible by virtue of its impossibility. Conversely, forgiveness is impossible – which is precisely what makes it possible.

This is not just a silly play on words, but a deep insight into a fundamental human phenomenon. It expresses what is meant by the philosophical term *aporia*. The concept, which stems from the Greek word for puzzlement, signifies a form of deadlock or stalemate. Only by action can the deadlock be broken – not by conducting even more analyses. In other words, we must forgive. According to Derrida, forgiveness (if genuine) has no purpose, justification or end. It cuts through all calculations about what has utility value and purpose – it is, as per this book's basic concept, an end in itself. If forgiveness becomes a means to something other than itself, it is no longer forgiveness.

In his text on the subject, Derrida discusses in depth the reconciliation processes in post-apartheid South Africa and other places as part of the process of rebuilding a nation. Derrida is certainly not opposed to such processes, however he believes it is misguided to talk about forgiveness in this context. He argues that if the forgiveness is instrumentalised in order to boost social cohesion or stop revenge attacks, then it succumbs to transactional logic – in other words, we forgive in order to get something back. Actual forgiveness – i.e. of the unforgivable – is not given in order to receive something in return. It is given unconditionally. Asking why is not meaningful. It is almost impossible to answer a question like this without making forgiveness instrumental and annulling any meaning as such. We may wish to forgive in order to feel better about ourselves, to repair a relationship or to 'move on', but in that case the forgiveness is conditional upon an external purpose, and is thus, according to Derrida, no longer forgiveness. The existence of unconditional forgiveness (as claimed by Derrida) serves to verify the existence of phenomena that cannot be justified by anything other than themselves, and thereby defies instrumental logic. Actual forgiveness is also, therefore, quite provocative. It challenges ordinary perceptions of what is reasonable. When the satirical magazine *Charlie Hebdo* published its first edition after the terror attack on it in 2015, the front page proclaimed 'Tout est pardonné' (All is forgiven). It was a radical, almost startling response. It might also be called an ethical response. Although it may at first appear weak because it does not seek revenge, it actually reflects incredible strength. The example also shows that only the injured party can forgive. It would not make sense for the President of the Republic, for example, to forgive the terrorists. Only those who have been attacked or offended against possess that power.

It is not just forgiveness that is *aporic* by nature (i.e. has the character of *aporia*, or paradoxical puzzlement). Derrida's famous analysis of hospitality is analogous – we can only be hospitable to the unwelcome. If somebody is invited, welcome and wanted, there is no reason to be hospitable. Hospitality entails the person who opens up their home voluntarily relinquishing control over their own space when they say to their guest 'make yourself at home!' We could also take a religious aporic example and say that it is only possible to believe in the unbelievable. If something is credible (for example,

2 + 2 = 4, or that London is the largest city in the British Isles), it takes no effort to believe it. We call it knowledge. Belief in virgin birth or eternal life is completely different, and is, therefore, a matter of faith. These phenomena also defy instrumental logic. We should not be hospitable to achieve something specific, e.g. being more popular, nor should we hold religious beliefs in order to be healthy and live longer, even though there appears to be a statistical correlation. We should be hospitable to be hospitable. Believe to believe. And forgive to forgive.

Derrida's analysis of forgiveness teaches us two things. Firstly, that genuine forgiveness is unconditional. It cannot be a means to something other than itself without ceasing to be forgiveness. Secondly, only the unforgivable can be forgiven. The forgivable can be accepted and understood, but not forgiven. Conversely, actual forgiveness – like that of Malmros – can be difficult to accept and impossible to understand. Nowadays, our understanding of interpersonal affairs is often based on reciprocity and symmetry (something-for-something). The notion of forgiveness defies this in a way that is perhaps more clear-cut than with any of the other existential standpoints presented in this book. Derrida imagines someone saying 'I will forgive you on the condition that, when you ask for forgiveness, you have changed and are no longer the same' – but forgiveness is impossible as soon as conditions are attached.

The incomprehensibility of forgiveness makes Derrida describe it as 'the madness of the impossible'. It might also be called ethically grounded madness, which is something quite different from pathological madness. It is madness because forgiveness goes beyond utilitarianism's strict calculations and rationality. Almost all contemporary examples of what we call forgiveness differ from Derrida's, as they are rational and understandable. We are usually told to forgive in order to achieve something. For example, Jack Kornfield, a Buddhist and author of *The Beginner's Guide to Forgiveness*, is preoccupied with the idea that we must forgive because it is good for us. As his website says:

> Kornfield explores why forgiveness, personally and globally, is essential to our health and happiness, and how you can start using this timeless practice to transform emotional wounds into healing and understanding. With guided meditations and insights from the world's wisdom teachings, Jack shows how forgiveness can be practiced as a gift we give, not only to others, but ultimately to ourselves.[6]

As a starting point, there is nothing wrong with something positive being achieved by forgiveness. The question is whether we overlook the radical groundlessness of forgiveness if its value depends on whether we gain from it. Having said that, it is possible for forgiveness to have no end other than itself and yet turn out to have fruitful consequences. The Danish radio host Ayse Dudu Tepe talked about forgiving her violent father in a way that would probably resonate with Derrida. She was going to pick him up at the airport:

> As I stood and watched him standing there all alone in Kastrup airport, I had a real *WTF* sensation. It was late. He has no idea I was going to pick him up, and I could see just how lonely he was. It was so existential, because, when all is said and done, we are all alone. I've always seen him as grown-up, strong and the type who would use his fists, but suddenly he was so much more than that. I forgave him there and then – now and forever.

It wasn't about what he'd done to me. Of course, I
don't accept what he's done. It was just forgiveness of a
human being.[7]

This is unplanned, uncalculated and spontaneous forgiveness in the existential sense. It had no end in itself,
it just happened. It was not the result of a conscious
choice, but it nevertheless had positive consequences.
'In fact, it meant that I was able to get on with my life',
says Ayse Dudu Tepe. 'It was one of the best experiences of my life – forgiving without ever having wanted
to.' Her story is about trust, but it is also fully in line
with Murdoch's emphasis on the ethical significance
of paying attention, in that forgiveness is possible via
paying attention to the other as merely human.

Forgiveness and asymmetric ethics

Derrida's analysis involves a radical rejection of all reciprocity and symmetry in ethics. This rejection is also
seen in Levinas and in Løgstrup, whose analysis of the
ethical demand underlined its unconditional nature.
We should not do good deeds or forgive because we
expect the same of the other. We should not do good
in the hope of something good in return. We should
do it because it has meaning in itself. In *The Ethical
Demand*, Løgstrup wrote about the one-sided nature
of the demand: 'The demand derives its one-sidedness
from the understanding that the individual's life is a
continuous gift, so we can never end up in a situation
where we are able to demand something in return for
what we do.'[8] It is difficult to imagine a clearer way of

expressing this asymmetry – and it is hard to imagine anything being more out of step with the rampant social instrumentalisation of our age. The individual's life is a continuous gift, yes, but forgiveness and the other standpoints suggested in this book should not be understood as gifts to ourselves. That would reduce their value to the subjective satisfaction of needs and so overlook their inherent value.

9

Freedom

Freedom is not constituted primarily of privileges but of responsibilities.

Albert Camus (1913–60)

Few ideas have been discussed so intensely throughout history as the idea of freedom. The debate about freedom can be said to consist of two separate philosophical tracks. One is about free will. Do people have any capacity to perform acts of will, or are we just complex machines controlled by the laws of nature? Is the experience of acting freely – e.g. choosing from a menu or doing something as simple as lifting an arm – nothing but an illusion? It is surprising how many philosophers and scientists have defended determinism, i.e. the view that free will is an illusion. In the past, determinism was mostly inspired by arguments from physics (everything in the world is essentially physical material that functions according to the principle of cause and effect – and humankind is not exempt from this) and psychology (childhood experiences determine human choices). Today, however, it is more common to argue

from a neuro-scientific perspective, claiming that caus-
ally determined brain processes drive human behaviour,
making free will an impossibility.

What surprises me about the prevalence of this point
of view is that determinism may well be a credible
theory on a purely intellectual level, but it is completely
impossible to live our lives by it. Morality, the law and
democracy are all based to some extent on people being
responsible actors who possess freedom of will, which
justifies them being called to account for their deeds and
misdeeds. If nobody can ever act freely, it seems unfair
to penalise them (and also meaningless to praise them).
Of course, we might also say that the act of administer-
ing punishment is itself determined, and therefore we
perhaps should not be held responsible for unjust legal
practices – but this just further illustrates the absurdity of denying the possibility of free will. All sorts of
ways of behaving towards each other are based on the
idea that people in some (but not all) cases, are able to
act freely. In other words, they could have acted differently. In legal cases, the defence of unsound mind is
used if a person 'was not him/herself' when the crime
was committed, i.e. could not have acted differently and
thus should not be punished. To remove this existential
tenet – that we are able to act freely – is to undermine
life as we know it. Similarly, in the chapter on dignity,
I argued – with reference to Kant – that we cannot live
under the assumption that our actions are determined.
Existentially, we must presuppose freedom because
otherwise nothing has meaning. As Kant pointed out,
perhaps we can never ultimately determine whether we
truly have free will – but we can, in practice, *think* that
we are free. This is sufficient, since it means that we can

relate to each other as members of what he called the kingdom of ends, and thus we can live meaningful lives.

The second philosophical track does not concern freedom of will, but individual freedom. It is less concerned with metaphysical questions about the nature of the universe and whether it allows for free will, and to a greater extent revolves around a more political philosophical question about what it means to be a free human being. This question has long been asked and has more to do with general social developments – e.g. during the French Revolution, when people fought under the banner of 'liberty, equality and fraternity'. The American philosopher John Dewey (1859–1952) once remarked dryly that people have fought for many things in the name of freedom, but certainly never for the metaphysical freedom of the will.[1] Rather, they have often fought for a specific form of political freedom, including freedom of expression, religion, assembly and association. In this chapter, I follow this second philosophical track and examine freedom as an existential standpoint. It may be more tangible and political than the metaphysical track, but that does not make it easier to grasp. Almost everybody would agree that freedom has a fundamental value for humans, but there is no consensus on what freedom actually consists of. What kind of freedom is worth fighting for? What kind of freedom cannot be made into a means for something else? The answer to this question will inevitably be coloured by our view of the nature of humankind.

The tragic existentialist

Albert Camus is, for many reasons, an interesting figure to consider when talking about freedom. I am writing this on the anniversary of his tragic death in a car accident. Exactly fifty-five years ago, he chose to drive with his publisher in the latter's Facel Vega HK500 – a beautiful French sports car – rather than accompany his family on the train. An unused train ticket was found in his jacket pocket. His death can be seen as symbolic of a key theme in his philosophy: the absurdity of life. For Camus, nothing has meaning, and yet people strive constantly to create it, an endeavour ultimately doomed to failure. His philosophy – as expressed in his essays and famous novels, for which he also won the Nobel Prize for Literature in 1957 (the second youngest recipient, only outdone by Rudyard Kipling) – is about both the tragedy and the absurdity of life. He famously retold the Sisyphus myth. Every day, Sisyphus rolls a heavy stone up the mountainside, for no apparent reason, only to start again from scratch the next day. He just rolls it and rolls it – he is engaged in a task with no end, much like waiting for Godot in Beckett's play. While Camus sees Sisyphus' endless, meaningless labour as a metaphor for life, he also, perhaps surprisingly, imagines that Sisyphus is happy, because he accepts his fate with dignity. For Camus, whether or not life is worth living was a basic question. In his book on Sisyphus, he writes that there is only one truly serious philosophical problem: suicide. Determining whether life is worth living is philosophy's basic question.

Camus is sometimes lumped in with the godfather of

existentialism, Jean-Paul Sartre, but there are significant differences between them. Sartre rejected the idea
of human nature and thought that 'existence precedes
essence' – in other words, that people are unbound
by any truth about themselves and are free to create
themselves through their own choices and actions. As
we saw in the chapter on love, Sartre also believed that
the individual creates values through the very act of
choosing them. This is a form of radical choice – not
just a choice between A and B, but a choice of whether
or not it is meaningful to choose between A and B at
all. However, in contrast to Sartre's radical existentialism, Camus thought that values 'derive from man's
innate humanity' and that 'there are certain eternal and
universal values in human nature – even if these values
have not necessarily been fleshed out'.[2] Values are not
freely invented by the individual, but are related to
humankind in general. Camus' view of humankind is
therefore just as reminiscent of the Greeks (and their
identification of human nature, see Chapter 1) as it is
of Sartre. The story of the two leading French philosophers' relationship with each other is in itself dramatic.
Their friendship ended in rupture, in particular due to
the clash between Camus' resistance to – and outright
contempt for – all forms of totalitarianism, and Sartre's
support for communism.

If Sartre was a pure existentialist, Camus is perhaps
better described as 'a philosopher concerned with existence'. He resisted classification as an existentialist, but
his philosophical and literary work on the concept of
freedom shows that he shares at least one of the existentialists' themes. For the epigraph of this chapter, I have
opted for a quote about freedom from one of Camus'

lesser-known texts, the essay 'Bread and Freedom', which was published in a collection with the dramatic title *Resistance, Rebellion and Death*.[3] The essay collection focuses on Camus' political and activist side. Although the texts were written many years ago, in a different political climate, several of them are still relevant today, including the one about bread and freedom, which consists of a long defence of human freedom. It begins with a critique of two distorted versions of the concept of freedom. One is the 'Western' version (linked to Western Europe during the Cold War), which Camus compares to a widow who is offered an attic room with her cousin's family and is told that, of course she is welcome in the kitchen, but otherwise is left in no doubt that she should be seen and not heard. She has the freedom to move around, but has no influence on her own life, or the life of the community (family). She is there, but without really being there. The second view of freedom is what Camus calls 'Eastern' (linked to the communist Eastern Bloc). Here, the widow is simply locked in a cupboard and told that she will be able to get out in fifty years – by which time the ideal society will have been established and she will be duly rewarded for her endurance. Where the former represents a diluted version of freedom, the latter is obviously a totalitarian distortion of the concept. Camus is right in saying that almost all regimes and forms of governance in modern times have sought to legitimise themselves with reference to freedom. However, they have also often suppressed it, especially by emphasising the necessity of things like security or full employment. This is the schism between 'bread' (which here stands for the material necessities of human existence) and freedom. Can

we justify sacrificing freedom in the name of bread? Not according to Camus. Freedom must never be sacrificed.

At the end of the essay, Camus gives a short and more positive definition of the concept of freedom that may surprise those who only know him as an existentialist. He writes: 'Freedom is not constituted primarily of privileges but of responsibilities.'[4] A purer existentialist would perhaps think that freedom simply lies in the act – in doing what we want – which is then protected by a society that gives individuals rights and privileges to act. Camus does not mention rights, but asserts that it is responsibilities that make up freedom. *Liberté oblige*, as it were. When we talk about duty and obligation, we find ourselves in the realm of normativity, which is all about claims, demands and responsibilities. But how can freedom be based on duty? Peder Syv (1631–1702), a Danish clergyman and folklore collector, recalls an old saying: 'He is free who does not as he wants, but as he ought.' In other words, freedom does not consist of doing whatever we want, but doing that which is required of us.

The idea of freedom expressed by both Camus and Peder Syv is perhaps alien in our day and age, when most of us instinctively think of freedom as an opportunity to do what we want. But the problem with our modern concept of freedom is that if we always do what we want (in the sense of what we most feel like), then we are not really free, but slaves to our desires. In the chapter on Kierkegaard's view of the self, I argued that what distinguishes human beings is our ability to rise above our immediate impulses and preferences and evaluate them in the light of moral values. From this emerges the self as a relation that relates to itself. Freedom is

therefore linked to the possibility of creating distance from our desires, and possibly suppressing them if they are not worth achieving. Freedom is therefore linked to duty – the duty to not just live in the moment, as we are constantly encouraged to do these days by everything from advertising to life coaches (Just do it! Live in the present! *Carpe diem*! What exactly are you waiting for?), but to reflect on and evaluate our desires.

However, just as we can make too much of immediacy if we always act on every impulse that strikes us, we can also make too much of reflexivity if we are forever mulling things over and never actually doing anything. The same Kierkegaard who defined the self as a reflexive relation that relates to itself also criticised the 'reflection sickness' that can result from constant self-reflection. It is this reflection on duty that makes us pause for thought when we are in danger of merely living in the moment, and at the same time stops us from succumbing to endless navel-gazing. Nobody has a duty to do whatever they want just because they feel like it, nor does anybody have a duty to indulge in infinite self-reflection. We will not find freedom in these extremes, only opposing forms of unfreedom.

Two concepts of freedom

By linking the concept of freedom to duty, Camus allies himself with a long tradition of thinking positively about freedom. In this context, 'positively' means that freedom is given content – it is freedom *to* (do) something. Conversely, there is an equally long tradition of thinking negatively about freedom – the freedom

from (doing) something. The most famous philosophical text about freedom is probably 'Two Concepts of Liberty', by the British philosopher and historian Isaiah Berlin (1909–97), which expands upon this distinction.[5] Berlin does not claim that there is a correct concept of freedom – and only one – but focuses on clarifying the different meanings of the concept in order to facilitate more rational discussion about it in both political and everyday contexts. According to Berlin, negative freedom is when nobody prevents us from doing what we want. Conversely, we do not have freedom in this negative sense if anybody is stopping us from achieving a goal. He notes that negative freedom is not necessarily associated with democracy. In principle, it is perfectly possible to envisage a benign dictator who makes sure that their subjects are able, as far as possible, to realise their desires and goals – in other words, a society where nobody prevents the citizens from doing what they want. This is perhaps a weakness in the concept of negative freedom – that it does not take into account who determines what we want (to do). We are free if we are able to realise our desires, irrespective of whether they are instilled in us by a thoroughly commercialised market society or by a technologically capable dictator – as is the case in countless science-fiction stories.

Conversely, the positive concept of freedom is not about what we are free *from*, but about the freedom *to*. It is about who controls us and what we are free to do. Berlin also calls this freedom as self-mastery. We are free if we are our own master. This involves, among other things, being able to self-reflect and evaluate our own wishes and desires (cf. Syv and Kierkegaard on the self) and the duties so closely associated with freedom

(cf. Camus). The question is, of course, how we acquire self-mastery. The answer is that it is not possible to do so alone. We are interdependent beings, only capable of self-reflection and achieving a degree of autonomy within societies and communities (see the chapter on the self). Freedom – at least in the positive sense – is therefore posited on being part of some form of community. A child who does not grow up in a context where they are able to cultivate the necessary skills for thinking, reflecting and self-control cannot be free, because they cannot achieve self-mastery. Further, we all have a duty to take care of communities in which it is possible to cultivate these skills, provided we desire freedom that is. This brings us back to square one: freedom and duty are inextricably linked. There can be no real freedom without the obligation to safeguard the conditions that make freedom possible. Nor can there be a duty to do something that we do not have freedom to do ('ought implies can', as Kant put it).

On the instrumentalisation of freedom

How, then, is freedom faring these days? On the face of it, we are good at protecting negative freedom. We salute the individual's right to do what they want (as long as it does not harm others), and we condemn barriers that might be put in the way of the individual's realisation of their own desires and goals. In my opinion, this is completely justified, but perhaps only tells half of the story. If the positive version of freedom is also significant, we must also remember to protect those communities in which people are able to cultivate their capacity for self-mastery. One term for this is 'formation', i.e. a form of (ethical) rearing and education. If Camus, Syv and (to an extent) Berlin are right, people must be formed in relation to something other than themselves in order to be free. Freedom does not consist in constant circling around the self and our inner desires and wishes, but in consideration of where we came from and of what we are a part. To coin a phrase, freedom is not just about self-insight, but also about self-outsight. Berlin even writes that 'what I am is, in large part, determined by what I feel and think; and what I feel and think is determined by the feeling and thought prevailing in the society to which I belong'.[6] Freedom presupposes knowledge of the community or society, and of the traditions and history that make us who we are.

This form of (positive) freedom is under pressure these days, as we seem to think that the most important thing is to 'know ourselves', rather than knowing and understanding the contexts that form us. One way to put it is to say that we often neglect formation in favour of self-realisation. Perhaps we do this because we mistakenly believe that it actually gives us freedom (*from* the potential oppression of old traditions). However, this is to forget that freedom is also freedom *to* act, in an informed and committed way, in the communities that make it possible for us to be free individuals in the first place.

In recent years, we have at times seen an outright instrumentalisation of freedom, where it is not seen as an end in itself but as a means to create something different – happiness, well-being, productivity, etc. Companies and organisations increasingly assume that employees will be more productive if they are given freedom and if responsibilities are delegated to them, rather than assuming that being free has intrinsic value as an expression of basic human dignity. The particular problem with this attitude is that the value of freedom is made relative to something else (e.g. productivity), which means that it is only justified to the extent that it supports this value. What if it turns out that freedom does *not* lead to higher productivity? If the argument for introducing freedom was based on it being a means to precisely that end, then it would perhaps no longer be legitimate. In his essay, Camus unambiguously defends the intrinsic value of freedom. He rejects the notion that any degree of happiness and well-being can offset the lack of freedom in a society. He writes: 'even if society were suddenly transformed and became decent and comfortable for all, it would still be a barbarous state unless freedom triumphed'.[7] Freedom, Camus argues, must not be sacrificed for material wealth.

Freedom is many things. For the ancient Stoics, it consisted of *eliminating* the fruitless desire to achieve peace of mind. For Kant, it was about the ability to *control* desire in order to act in accordance with moral law. Today, many seem to believe that freedom consists of *realising* our desires and full potential – being able to do whatever we want. Following Camus' lead, I have argued in this chapter that freedom is closely related to duty. To use Berlin's terms, freedom is partly positive, since it is about having the capacity to be able to do what we ought to do. But it is certainly also negative – no matter how much self-mastery we may possess, we can never be truly free if we live in a prison or dictatorship – except at best in the spiritual or intellectual sense. Regardless of how it is defined, it is worth standing firm on the fact that freedom has an intrinsic value that ought not to be instrumentalised by declaring that freedom is good *if* it promotes happiness or boosts GDP. Freedom is a good thing *per se* – even if it does not lift our spirits or benefit the economy. In that sense, it is an existential standpoint, an end in itself, on which it is worth standing firm.

10

Death

He who has learned to die has unlearned to serve.
              Michel de Montaigne (1533–92)

It is only fitting to round off with death. Unlike with the other standpoints in the book, I do not, however, mean to imply that death is an end in itself. To assert such a thing would be strange and perhaps nihilistic – a way of romanticising death, and something I would not endorse. Nonetheless, death can be considered a kind of meta-standpoint that serves as a frame or backdrop for the others, in parallel with Aristotle's highlighting of the good as an end in itself, as described in Chapter 1. As emphasised in the existential tradition – most notably by Martin Heidegger (1889–1976) – it is the acknowledgement of our finitude that confers meaning in life, or at least more meaning than anything else.[1] If there is nothing in life – for example the standpoints I describe in this book – that is more meaningful or important than other things, then everything becomes 'much of a muchness', because everything is equally important and therefore equally unimportant.

Humans, like all other living creatures, are mortal, but we are also at once burdened and enriched by our knowledge of that mortality. No other creature has an awareness of death the way we do. This awareness is a burden – for some, it even leads to an all-consuming fear of our ultimate obliteration. But it also enriches us, because it means that we are able to relate reflexively to our own lives and ponder what is meaningful. If we were not mortal – or did not know that we are – everything would just happen without us understanding that not everything can be achieved in life. And if not everything is achievable, it is all the more important to think about what it is *worth* spending time on. In other words, without death, there is no existential meaningfulness.

I remember that as a child I was fascinated by death. I recall thinking that if we all die and disappear, then nothing really matters. Nothing means anything if life is ultimately finite. This is not so far removed from Woody Allen's thinking, as referred to in the Prologue. As an adult, I still understand this idea, but now I would turn it around and say that everything has meaning *because* we die. The very fact that we live within a finite horizon means that our experiences and actions in life can have meaning and value. The philosopher Hans Jonas (1903–93) said that mortality gives us a 'narrow gate' through which value can enter 'an otherwise indifferent universe'.[2] If we were invulnerable, immortal beings, virtues like courage, perseverance, self-sacrifice or loyalty would be unthinkable. Standpoints like dignity, love and forgiveness would make little sense. We cling, in the existential sense, to that which we value, but also to that which can be taken from us – ultimately, life itself. For Jonas, only finite creatures can have values. We might say that *mortality* is a prerequisite for *morality*.[3] In other words, acknowledging mortality is a prerequisite for understanding moral values. Similarly, Iris Murdoch wrote that 'a genuine sense of mortality enables us to see virtue as the only thing of worth'.[4] Death is not a virtue in itself but represents the limits of existence, and therefore provides a context for virtues, standpoints and meaning.

To philosophise and die

In the Prologue, I discussed several perspectives on philosophy, deriving from wonder (Plato), disappointment (Critchley) and education for grown-ups (Cavell). Now, we can add another, one that originates with Socrates and was echoed by the likes of Cicero (107–43 BC) in Rome and the hero of this chapter, the French Renaissance humanist Michel de Montaigne. The perspective is, quite simply, that philosophy exists to teach us how to die well.[5] Philosophy is essentially preparation for death. In the famous dialogue *Phaedo*, in which he takes his leave of both his friends and his life, Socrates says, 'Those who are conversant with philosophy in a proper manner, seem to have concealed from others that the whole of their study is nothing else than how to die and be dead.'[6] Later, he adds: 'those who practice philosophy in the right way are in training for dying and they fear death least of all men'.[7] What does he mean by that? This brings us back to the idea of philosophy as a way of life, which I introduced at the start of the book. It consists of enquiry into the meaning of life and of living in accordance with human nature (which Aristotle called the virtues). But all of this is only important in the light of life's horizon or border – i.e. death. As the philosopher Todd May writes in his fine little book simply titled *Death*: 'Our mortality brings our lives shape; it gives those lives coherence and meaning. It makes the moments of those lives precious. And yet, dying threatens all that as well. It is good that we die, but never just yet.'[8] This is the paradox of death. Without it, nothing has meaning or value, but at the same time, death itself is a constant threat to precisely that meaning and value, as anyone who has lost somebody close to their heart will attest. Or, to put it another way, death is an existential condition of possibility for meaning, but is in itself meaningless.

To philosophise is to relate to this paradox. This is what Socrates means when he states that philosophy is training to die, and that one of its aims is to make us less afraid of dying. The Stoic philosophers in particular, including Seneca, Epictetus and Marcus Aurelius, who lived in the centuries after Jesus' birth, were particularly preoccupied with eliminating fear of death as far as possible through the daily reminder *memento mori* – remember that you must die! Reflecting on the ultimate negative and tragic aspect of life helps us become accustomed to the idea, which is impossible if we constantly turn our backs on death and pretend it does not exist. Awareness of death is also a major theme in the existential philosophy of Kierkegaard and Heidegger, who believed that humankind can only truly *live* in relation to death. Heidegger called this *Sein zum Tode* (being-toward-death). I dealt with the whole concept in my book *Stand Firm*, which drew heavily on the Roman Stoics. In the following section, we will see how the humanist Montaigne approached death.

The philosopher in the tower

Montaigne, a noble in Bordeaux in the sixteenth century, enjoyed an unusually rounded and humanist upbringing and education. In 1571, on his thirty-eighth birthday, he retired from public life and isolated himself for ten years in his tower in Château de Montaigne. The tower housed his library of more than 1,500 books – an incredible number for the time. It still stands, incidentally, and is open to the public. He immersed himself in his books and the world of ideas, and in 1580 published the famous work *Essais*, which means 'attempt' or 'draft'. In doing so, he invented the essay genre, combining the personal and anecdotal with the cultural and existential in an inspiring and experimental way, which allows the reader to follow the development of a thought without it necessarily reaching a definitive conclusion. The essayists of today would not write as they do had Montaigne not ensconced himself in his tower and written his 'draft'. The book represents a kind of nomadic thinking, in which Montaigne wanders from topic to topic (one essay is about cannibals, another about loneliness) with the explicitly formulated intention of describing humankind – using himself as the object of his studies – with unconditional candour. In this sense, he was the forerunner of today's autofiction writers, like Karl Ove Knausgård. After the publication of his essays, Montaigne left his tower, returned to public life and started to travel around Europe.

He even served as Mayor of Bordeaux. He died in 1592.

Essay number 19 in *Essais* carries the Socratic title: 'That to Study Philosophy is to Learn to Die'.[9] It is from here that the quote at the start of this chapter originates. Here is a slightly longer quote from the same essay:

> Where death waits for us is uncertain; let us look for him everywhere. The premeditation of death is the premeditation of liberty; he who has learned to die has unlearned to serve. There is nothing evil in life for him who rightly comprehends that the privation of life is no evil: to know how to die delivers us from all subjection and constraint.

The idea is interesting and intellectually challenging. We usually think of death as a limitation. Death limits life and thus our ability to live our lives freely. But for Montaigne, the opposite is the case – only if we understand death correctly can we be free. In his words, 'he who has learned to die has unlearned to serve'. If we do not learn to understand death and acknowledge its meaning, we may perhaps waste our lives on unimportant things without understanding the brevity of life. This makes us slaves of random, fleeting impulses, and unable to consider life from a more universal perspective. Just after the passage above, Montaigne goes on to describe an ancient Egyptian practice in which a symbol of death, e.g. a human skeleton, would be on display at their lavish banquets. According to Montaigne, a servant would then proclaim: 'Drink and be merry, for such shalt thou be when thou art dead.' Inspired by the Egyptians' embracing of death, Montaigne then articulates a maxim for life: 'so it is my custom to have death not only in my imagination, but continually in my mouth'. Simon Critchley concludes from this curious phrase that for Montaigne,

> To philosophize, then, is to learn to have death in your mouth, in the words you speak, the food you eat and the drink that you imbibe. It is in this way that we might begin to confront the terror of annihilation, for it is, finally, the fear of death that enslaves us and leads us towards either temporary oblivion or the longing for immortality.[10]

Only by confronting death head on and talking openly about it – as Montaigne puts it, by having death 'in your mouth', in the form of words and sentences – can we learn to live freely and without being paralysed by anxiety. We may not be able to rid ourselves of the fear of death, but we can learn to live better with it. For Montaigne, this is a prerequisite for freedom. Montaigne concludes by talking about his own fascination with death, and expresses a desire to create a catalogue of different ways in which people have died.[11] His aim is not to glorify death, but to rejoice in life. He writes: 'he who should teach men to die would at the same time teach them to live'.

We all die – so what?

The second-century Greek satirist Lucian of Samosata offers a moving description of human existence in his dialogue *Charon*. The title is also the name of the main character in the story, the ferryman who sails the dead to Hades. Only, in Lucian's tale, Charon is enjoying a well-deserved day off and is allowed to visit the realm of the living. With the help of Hermes, who is both messenger of the gods and the one who guides the souls of the dead to Hades, he piles mountains on top of each other in order to watch people from a high altitude. As he observes them, he reaches the conclusion that all living people have one thing in common: whether they are rich or poor, their lives are full of suffering. Charon concludes: 'If only they would start with a clear understanding that they are mortal, that after a brief sojourn on the earth they will wake from the dream of life, and leave all behind them, they would live more sensibly, and not mind dying so much.'[12]

Running through the thinking of Socrates, Lucian, the Stoics and Montaigne is this interest in death as something that should remind people of the importance of living here and now. *Memento mori* is important, as it impels us to *memento vivere* ('Remember that you must live!'), as Goethe put it in his novel *Wilhelm Meister's Apprenticeship* (1795). The idea lives on today in self-help literature and *carpe diem* tattoos. Sofia Manning, a well-known Danish life coach and student of Tony Robbins, starts her book *Hvad venter du egentlig på?* (What are you really waiting for?) with a reflection on the *memento mori* idea:

> Everything that seems so enormously important to you now will disappear. Everything that you have had and want to achieve, all your relationships, your daily dramas, obstacles and worries will disappear along with you. So why spend your short life sabotaging yourself? You are like a firefly in the night. Your life flares up briefly, and then you are gone. This is one of the most inspiring thoughts of all in the world. You are here for

a short and intensive period. Why not use life to the full while you are here?

Manning talks about her own brother's death, and how the loss made her aware that we should live life to the fullest while we still can.

Although she expresses the old *memento mori* idea, her conclusion is almost the complete opposite of that of the ancient philosophers. Manning believes that we must act *now*, because it may all be over at any moment. For her, coaching is a tool by which individuals can 'live out their dreams to the full'. According to her website, coaching will enable us to replace our 'inhibiting convictions (the thoughts and ideas that slow you down) with motivational and performance-enhancing convictions'.[13] These ideas seem to be the opposite of the philosophical life, the focus of which is not about 'living out our dreams to the full', but about examining whether our dreams are actually *worth* having, given the brevity of life and what it means to be human. My comments here are not in themselves an argument against coaching. Rather, I simply find it remarkable that the typical contemporary response to *memento mori* is 'Hurry up! Identify your dreams! Remove the inhibitions that prevent you from realising them!' It is so far removed from the philosophical response, which calls for peace of mind and reflection. 'What are you actually waiting for?' asks the coach eagerly. To which the philosopher would calmly answer: 'For death'. I may well be over-interpreting, but it is hard not to see the coach's starting point – 'What are you actually waiting for?' – as an instrumentalisation of death itself. Awareness of death becomes that which drives the individual to realise their dreams. I recently came across an even clearer example in *The New York Times*, in an article by the entrepreneur Arthur C. Brooks titled 'To Be Happier, Start Thinking More About Your Death'.[14] To this, I would respond: No. That is not why we should think about our death. We should think about our death because it is the horizon for meaning in life. If this thought makes us happy, that is fine. But the idea itself has meaning on its own.

In this chapter, I have argued that death is a prerequisite for anything in the world having intrinsic meaning and value. Death is hardly likely to make us happy, but it should be seen as a reality and as a condition of possibility for meaning. The old, 'useless' philosophers, of whom Montaigne is another example, would insist that, if we relate in the right way to this unavoidable condition, death can lead the way to a form of existential freedom. Death is not a standpoint as such, but a prerequisite for the existence of standpoints. It is not in itself meaningful, but a prerequisite for meaning.

Let me conclude with the Danish poet Grethe Risbjerg Thomsen's (1925–2009) brief poem about the importance of death and its constant presence throughout our lives.[15] For Thomsen, death is a process that begins at birth and does not stop at the end of life.

Maybe a March Night

I die a little
with every passing second.
I carry death in me
through years of life.

Death

One night, maybe in March,
mild with rain and thaw,
I will go into the darkness
and stop dying.

Epilogue: Perspectives on the Meaning of Life

I began this book with Woody Allen's assertion that life is meaningless. According to him, we are part of a purely physical universe that is ultimately doomed to perish, and therefore life has no meaning. Unlike Allen, I do not think that the former necessarily means that the latter is true. In my opinion, it is perfectly plausible to subscribe to modern physics' theories about the origin of the universe and its eventual demise – including evolutionary biology's teachings about the evolution of humankind (and its possible extinction) on Earth – without reaching the dramatic conclusion that everything is meaningless. This would be tantamount to concluding that nothing in this book has meaning because the letters are just black ink on white paper, and reflect light in a particular way due to the chemical properties of the ink. While I do not deny that some readers may find this book meaningless, I would venture that such an appraisal would not be due to the physical or chemical characteristics of the light and the ink, but because of *the content*. It is the content we need to discuss when we consider the meaning of a book, a poem, a law, an action or a human life. The starting point for this book is that, nowadays, we lack an understanding of the content and purpose of our activities, but we have become experts in the means and the instruments. We have become good at measuring and weighing the world, but bad at assessing the value of what we measure and weigh. We have developed means to optimise children's reading skills and adults' productivity, but we have lost the ability to discuss the content of what children read and the value of what adults produce. We calculate and conduct cost-benefit analyses of all sorts of things – at national level and in our own lives – to get the most 'bang for our buck', but find it difficult to discuss the meaning of our activities. This book uses the term *instrumentalisation* to describe this problem. The implication is that the focus is on means rather than ends, and that means have inappropriately been turned into ends in themselves.

The proposed solution is to embrace phenomena and activities that have intrinsic value. From a modern instrumentalist perspective, this may sound useless – but, paradoxically, it is a particularly useful form of uselessness. I have tried to show that throughout the history of philosophy, there has been an underlying idea that to adopt philosophy as a way of life is to resist instrumentalisation. At first glance, this may sound as if I am instrumentalising philosophy – making it a means to a meaningful life. However, that would be a misunderstanding, since my argument is that philosophical reflection on the value of things has its own inner meaning. The philosophical life is both a means to meaning and an end in itself – just like that which Aristotle dubbed *eudaimonia*.

Dialectic of Enlightenment

Criticising instrumentalisation is by no means new. One of the most famous cultural-analytical critiques of social instrumentalisation is *Dialectic of Enlightenment* by Theodor Adorno (1903–69) and Max Horkheimer (1895–73), two sociologically minded philosophers from the school of thought known as critical theory.[1] Critical theory is a philosophically inspired analysis of the dominant ideologies in a given society. Written during the Second World War and first published in 1947, the book seeks to analyse the rise of totalitarianism in Europe (especially, of course, in the form of the Nazis). How could the European Enlightenment ideas about science and human rights degenerate into awful terror regimes in only a couple of centuries? Modern science, with all of its medicine, technology and educational theory and practice, was supposed to have empowered people and liberated us from the monotonous drudgery of feudal society – but we ended up with world wars and the Holocaust. Like the later Holocaust analyst and sociologist Zygmunt Bauman,[2] Adorno and Horkheimer asserted that totalitarianism's horrors do not represent a reversion to a pre-modern barbarism, but are a consequence of modernity itself. Modernity's reason and faith in progress transform all too easily into a totalitarian dream of a utopian society, the pursuance of which justifies any means. According to Adorno and Horkheimer, modernity and enlightenment demystify the world, i.e. they destroy the old myths via science and technology, but the process is ultimately self-defeating. We may well acquire dominion over nature – including human nature – but we do not know what to do with this position of dominance, because we have no sense of the values that should guide our actions. Via this demystification, everything becomes a means rather than an end in itself.

The sociologist Max Weber (1864–1920) coined the term disenchantment, which is analogous to my use of demystification above. It refers to what I have described in this book as the process of the gradual disappearance of meaning in the outer world – and a corresponding 'enchantment' of the inner world, in the form of psychologisation and stressing the subjective. In Adorno and Horkheimer's words, reason becomes an 'instrument of an all-encompassing economic machine' in the modern demystified era.[3] This makes it difficult to grasp the idea that something may have intrinsic value, and everything thus becomes a means to something else. This presents a considerable challenge to reason – which knows that purpose, meaning and value exist. The dialectic of enlightenment robs reason of its beauty, reducing it to instrumentalism, cost-benefit analyses and utilitarian calculations. The ultimate consequence of this, as I argued at the beginning of the book, is nihilism: both active nihilism, as exemplified by the Nazis (and other contemporary totalitarian ideologies); and passive nihilism, in all those who believe that meaning necessarily comes from 'within' and is purely subjective.

Thankfully, despite the various crises of our era, this book was written under less dramatic circumstances than *Dialectic of Enlightenment*. However, in my opinion, criticism of instrumentalisation and nihilism is still highly relevant. Since the Second World War, we have increasingly made 'the market', the competition state, optimisation and performance into unwarranted ends in themselves. I have chosen to criticise this in a consciously edifying way, by constantly referring to the oases of meaning in life, to show that phenomena with intrinsic value still exist. I have identified ten existential standpoints – ten old ideas – but the list could have been much longer. I could, for example, have included play, trust, knowledge, democracy, education, friendship and art (although some of these are mentioned as examples under the various headings in the book).[4] The ten standpoints have special significance for me, but others will see things differently. I do not expect everyone to agree on what has intrinsic value. It is certainly a good thing if, in an open society, we are able to discuss what ought to be considered meaningful standpoints. In this sense, democracy and democratic conversations themselves form a significant standpoint, as they facilitate collective reflection on the general question of standpoints. This question is perhaps particularly relevant in relation to schools and education, which in recent years have been under particular threat from extreme top-down instrumentalisation, at the expense of developing students into citizens capable of engaging in informed discussions with others about meaning and value. The risk is not that we will disagree about standpoints – pluralism is good and desirable – but that too many of us will conclude that there is no meaning other than that which stems from the individual's subjectivity (psychologisation) or from pure means and market-oriented thinking (instrumentalisation). In both scenarios, the collective human, existential and moral issues are disregarded. Instead, the attention is focused solely on the means for realising the individual's wishes and preferences on the one hand, and social optimisation and demands for performance on the other.

Four perspectives on meaning

In the interests of pluralism, I will conclude by presenting four general perspectives on meaning, which are represented in this book in different ways and to different degrees. I will not attempt to hide where I stand, but would say that all four perspectives have some merit. The four perspectives are illustrated below in matrix form. The horizontal axis concerns whether meaning, in simplified terms, is about *experiences* (feeling good) or *actions* (doing good).[5] The vertical concerns whether meaning stems primarily from the *particular* or the *universal* in people.

The meaning of life	The experience dimension: feeling good	The action dimension: doing good
The particular: becoming yourself (self-development)	Hedonism	Nietzsche
The universal: becoming human (upbringing/ education)	Utilitarianism	The ethics of duty and virtue

For each of the four potential outcomes, I will present examples of currents of thought that hopefully illustrate these perspectives. Let us start in the upper-left quadrant, which perhaps represents the most common perspective in contemporary culture, where the meaning of life is taken to mean enjoying things, the quality of which can only be judged by the individual themselves. In other words, life is about experiencing as much as possible before we die, and the individual is sole arbiter of the value of what he or she experiences. I have placed hedonism here because it is a philosophy that stresses pleasure as the focal point of life. Just as we say that taste is not up for debate, for hedonists this principle applies universally, to every aspect of life. If *I* think that the meaning of life is to watch *The X-Factor*, precisely because it gives me the greatest enjoyment, then it *is* the meaning of life – for me. Others may certainly have other preferences, but they cannot correct me rationally. According to this thinking, I am allowed, first and foremost, to be myself as a unique, authentic individual and to explore my innermost desires. This quadrant quickly becomes subjectivistic, and any ideas regarding objective or common human values or duties become suspect. Large parts of the self-development industry depend on this way of thinking. For them, life is about identifying the individual's preferences and then, as far as possible, realising them (e.g. through coaching, therapy or other self-development tools). In this quadrant, the meaning of life consists of finding out what we *actually* want – so we can *just do it!*

In the field underneath this one, we find a kind of 'socialised hedonism', in the form of utilitarianism. Utilitarianism is a moral and value-based philosophy, which claims that an action is good if it maximises happiness (the individual's pleasure or satisfaction) for the greatest possible number of people. Like hedonism, the focus is still on the individual and their experience, but the difference is that it is deemed morally good that as many of us as possible enjoy the best possible experiences in life and realise our desires. Utilitarianism, too, is close to instrumentalisation, because nothing is good *per se* other than the individual's subjective experiences (of happiness and unhappiness). Everything else is considered a means to increase happiness and minimise unhappiness. However, utilitarianism may also include an element of education, as the cultivation of individuals who are mindful of others' wants and needs is a prerequisite for good citizenship. Although utilitarianism, in my opinion, is highly problematic as a form of axiology (the technical term for the study of values), there is good reason to retain elements of its underlying rationality, which it shares with hedonism. A meaningful life undeniably *also* consists, to some extent, of positive experiences – it ought to go without saying that a modern health service should evaluate the best way to deploy its resources to benefit the maximum number of patients, for example. The problem arises when we make subjective experience the *only* relevant consideration in life. As we shall see below, this is unsustainable, and leads to subjectivism and psychologisation.

In the upper-right-hand corner of the matrix of meaning is Nietzsche, who represents the view that meaningful life is created individually, through the strong loner's will to live and to create. For Nietzsche, in the wake of the death of God, there is no collective horizon of meaning on which to draw, so individuals must create their own meaning through their actions. Nietzsche despised experience-based philosophies that sought to create happiness, leading him to pen the famous words: 'Man does not strive for happiness, only the Englishman does that.' He was referring to the British utilitarians, who believed that all value could be calculated quantitatively in order to maximise happiness. Reading Nietzsche, we get a sense that life is characterised by depth and intellect, albeit linked exclusively to the will and abilities of the individual. His philosophy is elitist and intellectually aristocratic. This, as I have argued throughout this book, is perhaps a more correct approach to meaning and value than more experience-oriented philosophies – but it too is subjectivist, since it denies the existence of actual and given sources of meaning outside, and independent of, the individual.

These sources are, however, addressed by the fourth and final quadrant, in which meaning is linked to life as part of a human collective, with all the obligations and actions that entails. Despite significant differences, both the ethics of virtue (beginning with Aristotle) and the ethics of duty (in, for example, Kant) focus on this dimension. According to both traditions, certain things are meaningful and valuable for reasons arising not from the individual's subjectivity, but from human nature (Aristotle) and reason (Kant). Meaning and value are not defined by their potential to provide positive experiences, but as things that exist *per se*. The hedonist says that an action is good because they like it. The utilitarian says that an action is good because it creates good experiences for as many people as possible. Aristotle would say that we ought to learn to like doing good *because* it is good. And Kant would add that an action is good when it is performed out of respect for an objective morality, as humankind has an inherent dignity and should not be reduced to a means for anything whatsoever. In other words, it is in the lower-right quadrant that we find the strongest position from which to confront instrumentalisation. However, as mentioned previously, from my pluralistic perspective, this does not mean that the other fields are totally invalidated. It just means that they have not fully engaged with the nature of meaning, because they lack the crucial insight that there are aspects of human life that can be ends in themselves.

The experience dimension fails to take account of the fact that happiness is not necessarily the same as meaning. As Kant wrote in the *Fundamental Principles of the Metaphysics of Morals*, quoted from in Chapter 2: 'a happy person is something completely different from a good person'. As per Beckett, also cited earlier, we are still waiting for Godot, even when we are happy. It is meaningful to want to be a good person – even if it conflicts with our subjective well-being. Many freedom fighters, martyrs and altruists have lived lives that have been meaningful because they fought for common human values, even though it meant compromising on their subjective happiness. Conversely, it is possible to imagine a happy but psychopathic dictator who transgresses against common human values and therefore does not live meaningfully in the sense propounded in this book. Unfortunately, it is a part of the human tragedy that the morally good and meaningful life is not always rewarded with happiness and well-being. This provides all the more reason to admire those heroes and heroines whose good deeds came at the expense of their own happiness.

Welcome to the experience machine

To conclude, I would like to mention a famous philosophical science-fiction story designed to convince the reader that, in discussions of meaning, the action dimension in the table above should take precedence over the experience dimension. The story was written by the philosopher Robert Nozick (1938–2002) and included in his book *Anarchy, State and Utopia*.[6] I have adapted it slightly for the present context.

Imagine that scientists have invented an experience machine – a supercomputer that plugs into the central nervous system via a sophisticated interface. When plugged in to the machine, people experience exactly what it is that makes them most happy and contented. The computer can be programmed to suit the individual. A football fan can play for his country, win the World Cup and go on to be a successful manager of the national team. Someone else might be a world-famous concert pianist or win the Nobel Prize for curing cancer. Or, at least, they *experience* these things. The point is that the experience is so lifelike that they do not question the reality of it. Once plugged in, they forget that they are linked to the experience machine. And the process is so complex that it cannot be reversed – once they plug in, they cannot be unplugged again. Once they are in the machine, they are always in the machine – but they are guaranteed the most eventful and pleasurable life possible. In short, they are guaranteed happiness.

The question, then, is whether we would really want to be plugged into such a machine. Anyone who has seen the Matrix films (the first of which came out around twenty-five years after Nozick's book) will be familiar with the idea. Pessimists might argue that, in our media society, which constantly stimulates us through the internet and television, we already live in an enormous, collective experience machine. But it is still possible to go for a walk in the woods without our smartphone – unlike if we were plugged into Nozick's machine. Personally, I know that I would never sign up for the machine. Nor would anyone else with whom I have discussed the question. But why not? One argument I often hear is that we need to have encountered hardship and misfortune to appreciate good fortune and happiness, whereas the machine provides only happiness. But this is not a valid objection, because the machine could be programmed to deliver an optimal balance between good fortune and misfortune, misery and happiness, in a way that (as per the utilitarian view) maximises happiness.

I think that a better reason to say no is that the machine only delivers the experience dimension mentioned above. It delivers maximum happiness, but no meaning, because it offers no real opportunity to act (only the *experience* of acting). We achieve subjective happiness, but not the opportunity to do anything that might help us realise more objective human values. There is a difference between *living* a life and *experiencing* a life, and the machine allows only the latter. My contention is that the vast majority of us would choose real life – with all its uncertainty, hardship, suffering *and* potential for meaningful activities – rather than any 'experienced life', even if the latter comes with a guarantee of happiness. However, if we define happiness on the basis of experiences and assert that happiness is the highest value, then there is no reason *not* to plug into the machine. We are guaranteed 'full bang for our buck'. So the fact that we are instinctively reluctant to plug into the machine indicates that, when it comes to the crunch, happiness is *not* the highest value. This echoes the conclusion drawn by Kant's ethics of duty. We would rather strive for a meaningful life – in real, binding relations with others – than achieve maximum experienced happiness. We can also choose to stick with the idea that happiness *is* the highest value, but reject the idea that it is defined by experiences. This is in line with the conclusion drawn by Aristotle and the ethics of virtue. As mentioned in Chapter 1, Aristotle describes the good life (*eudaimonia* in Greek) as a form of life that has meaning. Irrespective of whether we side with Kant or Aristotle, the conclusion is that the meaningful life cannot be understood on the basis of categories of experience. It must be understood on the basis of categories of action, where people engage in activities that have intrinsic value. It has been this book's errand to argue precisely for that – because it is a basic existential concept that is threatened by social instrumentalisation.

The ancient Greeks' perspective on the value of action is completely different to ours. One of the most dramatic illustrations of this is the tale of Kleobis and Biton told by the historian Herodotus (about 480–420 BCE). The story goes that the two brothers, sons of Cydippe, priestess of Hera, pulled their mother in a heavy cart for eight kilometres because the oxen had become too tired. When they finally reached their destination, the temple of Hera, the brothers fell asleep exhausted. Their mother, proud of her sons' achievement, prayed to the goddess to bestow on them the best gift a god might give a human. Hera, in all her divine goodness, heard the mother's prayer. And what happened? The sons never woke up again – they died in their sleep. This was their gift.

The moral of the story is almost incomprehensible to

us today, but in the context of ancient Greece, Hera did in fact bountifully reward Kleobis and Biton, because their lives were complete. Their self-sacrifice had been so noble-minded and morally good that whatever they might have gone on to do later would only have detracted from the moral quality of their lives. From a Greek point of view, Kleobis and Biton lived meaningful lives, despite not experiencing much that was good or exciting. The story reminds us that meaning and morality cannot be understood in purely quantitative, instrumental or experiential terms (e.g. by measuring happiness, health or subjective well-being). Rather, the moral and meaningful have intrinsic value. We must live morally because it is good to do so, not because it makes us happy or is healthy (although these days we may reasonably hope for a longer life than the two Greek brothers). The ten standpoints put forward in this book help us to reflect on what has intrinsic value in our lives – and show that old ideas can have meaning in a new and different world.

Notes

Prologue

1 Read the interview in full at: http://www.buzzfeed.com/ alisonwillmore/woody-allen-believes-that-life-is-meaning less#.xrrRgrxow.

2 See for example Niels Åkerstrøm Andersen's analysis of play as a management tool in *Legende magt* (Playful Power) (Hans Reitzels Forlag, 2008).

3 See, e.g., the analysis by the statisticians Svend Kreiner and Karl Bang Christensen, 'Analyses of model fit and robustness: a new look at the PISA scaling model underlying ranking of countries according to reading literacy', *Psykometrika*, 79 (2014), pp. 210–31.

4 The phrase was coined by Ove Kaj Pedersen in the book *Konkurrencestaten* (The Competition State) (Hans Reitzels Forlag, 2011).

5 This is described and discussed critically in several of my books, including *Stand Firm: Resisting the Self-Improvement Craze* (Polity, 2017) and S. Brinkmann and C. Eriksen (eds), *Selvrealisering – kritiske diskussioner af en grænseløs udviklingskultur* (Self-realisation: Critical

Discussions of a Development Culture That Knows No Boundaries) (Klim, 2005).

6 It goes without saying that it is somewhat simplistic to be so categorical about psychology as a whole, and laudable exceptions do exist. It should also be mentioned that it is relevant to differentiate between *psychology* (as a particular way of looking at people and their lives) and *psychologists*, who as a rule are very ethical and highly empathic individuals. My criticism is of psychology as, in Foucault's terms, 'a cultural form'. In other words, it is not so much a critique of scientific psychology, actual psychologists or the many excellent forms of treatment that have been developed, but of psychology as a way of interpreting life that has come to characterise Western culture. See Foucault's 'Philosophy and Psychology', in *Aesthetics, Method, and Epistemology: Essential Works of Foucault*, edited by J.D. Faubion (The New Press, 1998). In my own book *Psychology as a Moral Science: Perspectives on Normativity* (Springer, 2011), I attempted to present a far more in-depth analysis of psychology's lack of a normative foundation and the risk of instrumentalisation that this entails. This book's identification of existential standpoints, and its conceptualisation of the individual as a creature with obligations and relations to others, could be interpreted as a philosophical starting point for a general psychology that, in my opinion, is suitable for understanding human life.

7 The book was written by James Hillman and Michael Ventura and was published in 1992 by HarperOne. The point is that all of the empathetic, sensitive people who ought to be engaged in improving society are lying on therapists' couches and only improving themselves and discovering what is within them.

8 Stanley Cavell, *The Claim of Reason* (Oxford University Press, 1979), p. 125.

9 Pierre Hadot, *Philosophy as a Way of Life* (Blackwell, 1995).

10 See, for example, his *Infinitely Demanding: Ethics of Commitment, Politics of Resistance* (Verso, 2007).

11 This book is agnostic when it comes to the existence of a God. Perhaps there is one, perhaps not. Regardless of our view on this, secularisation forms the backdrop to discussions of society and life in general. In his major work *A Secular Age* (Harvard University Press, 2007), Charles Taylor – a practising Catholic, incidentally – defined secular society as one in which belief in God is not taken for granted, but is one option among many. In other words, a secular society may still have lots of religious people and practices, but the starting point is nevertheless completely different than in a society where religious ideas are taken for granted and unchallenged. Once religion is made a matter of choice, it is probably impossible to return to a pre-secular society.

12 In *A Significant Life: Human Meaning in a Silent Universe* (University of Chicago Press, 2015), Todd May argues that God is not *per se* a guarantor of meaningfulness.

13 Cited here from Darrin McMahon's *Happiness: A History* (Atlantic Monthly Press, 2006), p. 454.

14 Tania Zittoun accounted for the psychological and developmental importance of symbolic resources in her book *Transitions: Symbolic Resources in Development* (Information Age, 2006).

15 *Philosophy as a Way of Life*, p. 267.

Chapter 1 The Good

1 The article is on pages 42–44 and was written by Risto Pakarinen. You can find it at this link: https://scandinavi antraveler.com/sites/default/files/st1509.pdf.

2 See http://classics.mit.edu/Aristotle/nicomachaen.1.i.html.

'Some ends are subordinate to other ends, because the latter provide the motive for pursuing the former (e.g., the activity of bridle-making is subordinate to the more important activity of horsemanship, which is in turn subordinate to the activity of military science). The major ends for the sake of which minor ends are pursued are superior and ought to be preferred.'

3 This is also one of the main themes in Hadot's *Philosophy as a Way of Life*.

4 When forty-five minutes of exercise per day was introduced into the Danish school curriculum, one of the justifications was that it would improve children's mathematical and language skills.

5 As conceptualised under the heading 'the competition state'.

Chapter 2 Dignity

1 Karl Ove Knausgaard, *A Death in the Family*, translated by Don Bartlett (Harvill Secker, 2013), p. 3. This is followed by one of Knausgård's characteristic meditations, on the heart, blood and the body, which establishes the main theme of the book: death.

2 First published in German in 1785. *Fundamental Principles of the Metaphysics of Morals (Second Section)*, https:// ebooks.adelaide.edu.au/k/kant/immanuel/k16prm/chap ter2.html.

3 Ibid.

Chapter 3 The Promise

1 Friedrich Nietzsche, *On the Genealogy of Morality* (Cambridge University Press, 1994), p. 35. The following section is based on 'Guilt – the feeling of morality', which I wrote for the anthology *Hverdagslivets følelser*

(Everyday Emotions), edited by Michael Hviid Jacobsen and Inger Glavind Bo (Hans Reitzels Forlag, 2015).

2 This is one of the main themes in Sabina Lovibond's important moral philosophy book *Ethical Formation* (Harvard University Press, 2002).

3 *Manden der ville være skyldig.* English translation by David Gress-Wright (Marion Boyars, 1982).

4 In her book *Giving an Account of Oneself* (Fordham University Press, 2005).

5 Ibid., p. 85.

6 See Anders Fogh Jensen, *The Project Society* (Aarhus University Press, 2012).

Chapter 4 The Self

1 Søren Kierkegaard, *The Sickness Unto Death* (1849), http://www.religion-online.org/showchapter.asp?title=20 67&C=1863.

2 See, for example, the classic work by Vygotsky, *Mind in Society: The Development of Higher Psychological Processes* (Harvard University Press, 1978).

3 For example, Christian Hjortkjær of the Søren Kierkegaard Research Centre at the University of Copenhagen.

4 Most notably in his book *Sources of the Self* (Harvard University Press, 1989).

Chapter 5 Truth

1 Hans-Jørgen Schanz, *Handling og ondskab – en bog om Hannah Arendt* (Aarhus Universitetsforlag, 2007), p. 39.

2 Hanna Arendt, *The Human Condition* (Chicago University Press, 1998), p. 279.

3 Quoted in Hadot, *Philosophy as a Way of Life*, p. 212.

4 Henrik Høgh-Olesen, in the Danish newspaper *Politiken,*

available online (in Danish) here: http://politiken.dk/
indland/art4844460/De-fleste-lyver-heldigvis-hver-enes
te-dag.

5 Let me make it clear that I basically consider myself a
Darwinian. Darwin was a fantastic natural scientist, whose
observations and theories have proven to be correct. But
this is an entirely different conclusion to the one drawn
by some modern evolutionary psychologists, i.e. that the
Darwinian perspective is not only *necessary* but also *sufficient* to understand human existence. And that, I think,
is wrong. To proclaim that our convictions are solely
based on their utility value removes everything normative
from life. Another problem with this kind of reductionist
Darwinism is that belief in the theory itself ends up depend-
ing on whether adhering to it has survival value, which
means the theory runs the risk of being self-refuting. This
argument has been made by, *inter alia*, Thomas Nagel, in
his book *The Last Word* (Oxford University Press, 1997).

Chapter 6 Responsibility

1 On the origins of the book see, e.g., Kees van Kooten
Niekerk's 'Road to *The Ethical Demand*', in D. Bugge
and P.A. Sørensen (eds), *Livtag med den etiske fordring*
(Klim, 2007), which also contains a wealth of interesting
interpretations of Løgstrup's main ethical work.
2 K.E. Løgstrup, *Den etiske fordring* (The Ethical Demand)
(1956; Gyldendal, 1991), p. 27. Translations are from the
1991 Danish edition. An English edition, edited by Hans
Fink, was published by Notre Dame Press in 1997.
3 *Den etiske fordring*, p. 25.
4 Ibid., p. 37.
5 Ibid., p. 39.
6 Countless scientific sources could be quoted here, among
them Christopher Peterson and Martin Seligman's

Character Strengths and Virtues: A Handbook and Classification (Oxford University Press, 2004).

7 *Den etiske fordring*, p. 271.

8 Ibid., p. 33.

9 Richard Sennett, *The Craftsman* (Yale University Press, 2008).

Chapter 7 Love

1 'The Idea of Perfection' (1962), included in Iris Murdoch's *Existentialists and Mystics*, edited by Peter Conradi (Penguin, 1997).

2 'The Sovereignty of Good Over Other Concepts' (1967), in *Existentialists and Mystics*.

3 'The Sublime and the Good' (1959), in *Existentialists and Mystics*, p. 215.

4 'The Sovereignty of Good Over Other Concepts', p. 373.

5 Jens Mammen, *Den menneskelige sans* (The Human Sense) (Dansk psykologisk forlag, 1996).

6 'The Sublime and the Good', p. 215.

7 Carl Rogers, *Becoming Partners: Marriage and Its Alternatives* (Dell, 1970), p. 10. Rogers is an extremely important figure in psychology, whose significance is perhaps comparable to Freud. Though not as famous as the latter, Rogers' development of 'person-centred therapy', based on unconditional acceptance and recognition, is the direct precursor of many modern relational practices, such as coaching and appreciative inquiry.

Chapter 8 Forgiveness

1 Founded by the linguist Ferdinand de Saussure (1857–1913), structuralism went on to become an immensely influential perspective in twentieth-century philosophy, comparative literature and social science.

2 See, e.g. Critchley's *Book of Dead Philosophers* (Granta Books, 2009).
3 The interview is from 2013 and is available here (in Danish): http://politiken.dk/kultur/filmogtv/art5481507/ Nils-Malmros-%C2%BBHer-og-nu-var-der-ikke-andet-i-verden-end-at-redde-Mariannes-liv%C2%AB.
4 See http://www.kristeligt-dagblad.dk/kultur/hvor-der-ik ke-er-skyld-er-der-heller-ikke-brug-tilgivelse.
5 Jacques Derrida, *On Cosmopolitanism and Forgiveness* (Routledge, 2001), p. 32.
6 See https://jackkornfield.com/the-beginners-guide-to-for giveness.
7 *Ud & Se*, no. 11 (2015), p. 32.
8 *Den etiske fordring*, p. 141.

Chapter 9 Freedom

1 He made the remark in *Human Nature and Conduct* (The Modern Library, second edition, 1930), p. 303.
2 The quotes are from Jørn Boisen's excellent chapter on 'Camus og eksistentialismen' (Camus and Existentialism), in P.H. Amdisen, J. Holst and J.V Nielsen (eds), *Studier i eksistenstænkningens historie og betydning* (Studies of the History and Meaning of Ideas about Existence) (Aarhus University Press, 2009), p. 71.
3 Albert Camus, *Resistance, Rebellion and Death* (The Modern Library, 1963).
4 Ibid., p. 70.
5 'Two Concepts of Liberty' can be found in Berlin's *Four Essays on Liberty* (Oxford University Press, 1969).
6 Ibid., p. 157.
7 *Resistance, Rebellion and Death*, p. 66.

Chapter 10 Death

1 See, e.g., David Couzens Hoy's short essay 'Death', in *A Companion to Phenomenology and Existentialism*, edited by Hubert Dreyfus and Mark Wrathall (Wiley-Blackwell, 2009).

2 Hans Jonas, 'The Burden and Blessing of Mortality', *Hastings Center Report*, 22 (1992), pp. 34–40.

3 I argue this in the article 'Questioning Constructionism: Toward an Ethics of Finitude', *Journal of Humanistic Psychology*, 46:1 (2006), pp. 92–111.

4 'The Sovereignty of Good Over Other Concepts', in *Existentialists and Mystics*, p. 381.

5 See, for example, Cicero, 'Against Fear of Death', in *On Living and Dying Well* (Penguin Classics, 2012).

6 Plato, *Phaedo*, 64a (Taylor's translation).

7 Plato, *Phaedo*, 67e (Grube's translation).

8 Todd May, *Death* (Acumen, 2009), p. 76.

9 Available in English online: http://publicdomainreview. org/collections/that-to-study-philosophy-is-to-learn-to-die-1580.

10 *Book of Dead Philosophers*, p. xii.

11 Critchley's *Book of Dead Philosophers* is one such catalogue, detailing the deaths of almost 200 philosophers, providing insight into their thoughts and reflecting on death as part of our cultural history.

12 Quoted in Hadot, *Philosophy as a Way of Life*, p. 246.

13 See http://www.sofiamanning.com/index.php?pageid=01.

14 *New York Times*, 9 January 2016, http://www.nytimes. com/2016/01/10/opinion/sunday/to-be-happier-start-thin king-more-about-your-death.html.

15 From the collection *Dagen og Natten* (The Day and the Night) (1948).

Epilogue

1 Theodor Adorno and Max Horkheimer, *Dialectic of Enlightenment* (Verso, 1997).

2 Particularly in his book *Modernity and the Holocaust* (Cornell University Press, 1989).

3 *Dialectic of Enlightenment*, p. 30.

4 Various thinkers have drawn up other lists of elementary human values, e.g. Martha Nussbaum's list of basic human capacities (life; bodily health; bodily integrity; sensing, imagination, thought; emotions; practical reason; affiliation; other species; play; and control over one's environment). The conservative philosopher John Finnis lists seven 'basic human goods' – life, knowledge, play, aesthetic experience, friendship, practical reason and religion – based on what he considers to be natural law. As I do in this book, both Nussbaum and Finnis argue that the elements in their lists have intrinsic value and should be protected from instrumentalism and utilitarian relativisation. See, for example, Nussbaum's *Women and Human Development: The Capabilities Approach* (Cambridge University Press, 2000) and Finnis' *Natural Law and Natural Rights* (Oxford University Press, 1980).

5 The first distinction, between *feeling good* and *doing good*, is inspired by the Danish philosopher Jørgen Husted, who was my lecturer in the mid-1990s. See, for example, his *Wilhelms brev: Det etiske ifølge Kierkegaard* (William's Letter: The Ethical According to Kierkegaard) (Gyldendal, 1999).

6 Robert Nozick, *Anarchy, State, and Utopia* (Basic Books, 1974).